*To my daughter Carolyn
this book is lovingly dedicated*

"One Great Fellowship of Love" in the hymn *In Christ There
Is No East or West* designed by Margaret Taylor for a World
Day of Prayer in Athens Ohio and further described pp.54-5
(*photo by Darrell Tom*).

DRAMATIC DANCE WITH CHILDREN

In Education And Worship

MARGARET TAYLOR

editor, DOUG ADAMS

Illustrations by Ruth Baldwin

For inclusive imagery, one should reverse
the assignment of roles indicated in some
sections of this volume.

The Sharing Company

TABLE OF CONTENTS

PART THREE

CREATIVE DRAMATIC MOVEMENT

WITH FIVE - SEVEN-YEAR OLDS

RESOURCES AND ACKNOWLEDGEMENTS

Introduction

Christian learning involves participation in experiences that change the self, that illuminate and liberate the self. It means clarification of goals and insight for the struggles by which persons realize goals. It means understanding and love for the other persons without whom the individual is incomplete. It means all of these because it means a meeting with God—with the holy, righteous, loving God—who creates life and bids persons enter into fuller life.

—ROGER SHINN

Creative movement as a part of religious education has become significant in the opportunity it offers all students to correlate, interpret, and animate their spiritual, intellectual, and social interests. Through this form of art children love to express what they think, feel, and see. Children and teachers learn and share together through movement experiences.

As creative power is given opportunity for expression in terms of everyday experiences, a child responds with his own ideas in some form of movement expression. This movement may not possess greatness in form—which cannot be expected of a child—but the experience helps him to grow spiritually. Recognition, development, and encouragement of this creative power will lead to the enrichment of daily life.

Creative movement is motivated by feelings, beliefs, ideas, thoughts, experiences, people, situations, and all the other many aspects of living. Therefore, creative rhythmic movement in our educational system is not learning dances, nor a series of techniques, but a process that leads an individual to creative expression.

—MARTHA CORNICK

CREATIVE MOVEMENT IN CHRISTIAN EDUCATION

"Christian education aims at the development of the whole person—his specific needs, his relationships to other persons, his ways of communicating with them, his search for meaning in life, his acquisition of knowledge, his response to God, and his growing understanding of Christ. Creative rhythmic movement, or dramatic movement as it is often called, is an art that assists in the nurture of all these aspects of the growing person, and lends itself especially well to the Christian education of children."*

Creative dramatic movement can assist a child to express and discover:

how he might feel to be new at school and have another help him to be "at home" through expressive actions

how the story of the good Samaritan, for instance, could be dramatized through experimenting with the way each character might walk

how to drain off tensions and hostility through actions

how a hymn, carol, or spiritual might be expressed with meaningful motions while singing

* From *Time for Wonder* by Margaret Fisk Taylor, p. 10. United Church Press (The Christian Education Press), 1961.

how prayer may be more meaningful through the use of symbolic movements.

Although the material in this book is beamed mainly at leaders in Christian education (whether in church school, extended sessions, weekday sessions, junior choirs, vacation church schools or family camps), this material is useful for parents also, for Christian education is not a matter of class instruction, but a growing experience in the everyday life of the child. Virginia Tanner who is a leading teacher in creative movement writes: "The key to guiding [the] child to self-fulfillment lies in nurturing those daily moments which are potentially thinking, feeling, exploring experiences." In this day when parents feel that the children must take "this instruction" or "that class," they need to be reminded that the daily moments with their children are sacred moments to explore and discover together. Our culture is endangered by professionalism; the home must be real and deep and without any pretense. The total being of the child must be free to communicate with the parent in this sensitive growing period. And parents need to know of this use of dramatic movement as background understanding.

What Is Creative Dramatic Movement?

A child *discovers* as he takes time to explore how an idea might be expressed through using his total self—not only his thinking and his feeling, but also using his own expressive actions. This is creative dramatic movement. It allows a child time for discovery, for gaining fresh insight, for involvement in a total way —for this is an earmark of discovering: that one uncovers what existed before but remained unknown.

As in the Sioux Indian prayer: "Great Spirit, help me never to judge another until I have walked in his moccasins for two weeks," understanding is gained through doing; so through imagination linked with expressive movement the child makes new discoveries, for his understanding is expanding and deepening.

Creative movement should always be called "dramatic activity" or "dramatic movement," not "dance"—because it is simpler than what is considered dance—and not "rhythms"—because that term is often associated with activities of younger children, such as rhythm bands. Boys, as well as girls, are not afraid to experiment with "dramatic activities" and they are keen discoverers of ways to communicate through action. Even if children have had some dance training, it should be made clear that this dramatic movement is to be creative from their inner thinking and come out through their whole being. It is a discovering time, not a performing time.

Natural Movement

"Creative movement or rhythmic interpretation is an art of natural movement used to express and interpret ideas, insights, and moods. It may be experienced by an individual or a group. In its simplest form it may consist of bodily movement, often with a rhythmic pattern, as a spontaneous overflow of energy and feeling, or it may be more extensive, involving deep consideration, exploratory attempts at moving to communicate inner convictions, and the evolving of a pattern that is remembered

and repeated. It may be spontaneous or it may be worked out gradually."[*]

Individual creative dramatic movement evolves naturally through:

1. grasping an idea with imagination
2. portraying the idea by assuming a total dramatic posture as in "playing statues"
3. intensifying this dramatic portrayal by more contraction, more extension, or more of an angular twist
4. including active movement to prolong, to try variations, or to alternate with contrasting movements.

For example: How do you suppose the prodigal son felt when he was alone, caring for the pigs, discouraged, wanting to go home, but feeling that he should not?

a. Grasp this idea first with the imagination.

b. Take a posture he might have been in —total: head, shoulders, hands, back, legs, feet, even toes.

c. Intensify this posture: contrast much further into a discouraged lump, or extend like Rodin's "The Prodigal Son" in an agonized reach, or show contrast in some other way.

d. Motion: variation of reach and then contraction; reaching to different sides or elevations.

Remember what happened? He arose and started back to his father. Here is a contrast of dramatic movement!

The important matter is for the child to grasp an idea with imagination; the other items evolve naturally. The child will not forget about the prodigal son—he has had a chance to be totally involved.

What does the leader do? He helps in the first step; then stays in the background while each child experiments at his own speed. If some finish earlier than others, he quietly com-

---
[*] From *Time for Wonder*, p. 10.

10

municates to the child that he should remain still and observe the others. The leader encourages the children, sometimes mentioning an unusually creative idea and allowing time for the children to discuss verbally what new ideas they may have had. The teacher need not pry, but should allow time if some wish to speak. He can show pictures of sculpture or paintings of the prodigal, and the children can evaluate them, deciding which ones have meaning for them.

When children work as a *group* using dramatic movement:

1. They take time for individual creative exploration of movement as previously described.

2. They share ideas with each other, showing what actions they have improvised.

3. They choose harmonious (not unison) movements so that they may move as a group or as harmonious groups.

4. The leader encourages when movements communicate the ideas and urges new experiments when the movements are weak, sterile, superficial, or meaningless.

Helping Children Adjust

The child who is *not readily verbal* needs opportunities to communicate through dramatic action. To discuss and to read may be tiring to him, but to move is a release and he feels more identified with ideas and with others if there is some active participation instead of the use of words only.

Creative children often lag behind their age group in regard to verbal ability. "The exuberance and flexibility of the creative child are the surest sign of a healthy, fully functioning personality. It is not creativity but its suppression that parents need to worry about," writes E. Paul Torrance, researcher in education at the University of Minnesota. In Christian education today there is not nearly enough encouraging of creative outlets for the "exuberant" children. Creative dramatic movement is one of the natural arts that have been suppressed in our teaching beyond the nursery, kindergarten, and primary departments. Older children enjoy dramatic movement and have a great deal to discover through this art.

The *highly verbal* child is often tense, and overtalkative because of tension or insecurity, and he may be used to small and repressed movements. This child can find release, security, and clarification through dramatic action that involves his whole being. Instead of a glib chatter of words, the child is confronted with reaching into the real mood or underlying idea, and afterward his words have more depth and body. Honest involvement can remove the mask of multiple words and allow the illumination of creative action. Martin Buber has said, "When you utter a word before God, then enter into that word with every one of your limbs."

Children who are *retarded* find a natural and free use of movement to express their ideas and feelings. Here is an art where those less gifted may feel adequate and blend in well when involved with a general group.

Recently a group of children of the fifth, sixth, and seventh grades presented an interpretation of "For the Beauty of the Earth" in a morning service. One of the children was retarded, but there was no indication of this as she expressed her worship with the others.

Children who are *disturbed* find release and can communicate in more depth when they are free to use dramatic movement. This is a growing field in movement therapy. (As I viewed the motion picture *David and Lisa*, I kept thinking, "Lisa is so full of rhythm, she could dance out her answer if only she could be encouraged to do this." As Shakespeare wrote: "There is measure in everything . . . so dance out the answer.")

11

IF CREATIVE MOVEMENT IS NEW TO YOU

Because leaders have not used a creative dramatic approach as much as only verbal discussion, many are fearful or feel insecure about trying to discover its possibilities. So, much of the material in this book is written in the way one "might" encourage the start of expressive movement. *The child's natural response to ideas is to make some active response*—not just listen and discuss verbally. Some of this response action involves the face, hands, the whole body, the whole self. You, as leader, help the child to feel free to respond totally so that both he and you may discover further.

There are two Parts in this book but much of the material in Part One is usable with children in the older age-group (Part Two); much that is in the second part can be simplified for use with children in the younger age-group or adapted for use with junior high young people. So use the whole book as source material. On pages 73-74 is a listing of books and articles that offer background on the use of creative movement with children. A series of filmstrips on creative dramatic movement is listed also. These resources are included to urge you to explore with the children.

The book assumes participation by boys as well as girls. The boys appreciate having the leader be a man or the assistant, a man or older boy. Where men are in charge of children of this age the response from the boys is excellent. This is especially valuable in family camps where fathers enter into activities. To have men participate means that the boys are assured that this dramatic activity is not "sissy" business. A good leader, encouraging boys to do meaningful and strong actions, is effective, however, whether the leader is a man or woman.

Norma Lowder has written an entire article, "Music for Juniors," related to the use of *movement with music* for children of the junior department. She says:

All children will experience emotional release and body-soul training that more than warrants the inclusion of creative rhythms as a part of vacation church school, weekday extended sessions, or junior choir activity. . . . Children must know that you want them to express their feelings, rather than to reflect yours, and that you enjoy experimenting with movement. . . . The vital need of our children for spiritual expression can, to a large extent, be met through a well-planned program of creative rhythms.

Creative dramatic movement can be done in a limited area or in a large area, indoors or outdoors. If the area is small, portions of the group may use space in turns, while others are involved indirectly. If the area is large, limits should be set, especially when outdoors. It is ideal if the church has an outdoor area somewhat secluded from public passersby. In the summertime there may be access to a large backyard or there may be opportunities at family camps.

If creative movement is new to you and you feel that you need more help in getting started, read pages 10-18 of *Time for Wonder,* a basic book by the same author (United Church Press [The Christian Education Press], 1961), to which *Time for Discovery* is a companion book. *Time for Wonder* has suggestions for sessions with children of five, six, and seven years of age. The material in both books can be adapted for use with different age levels.

The leader is free to use or adapt any of the material offered in this book. He is also urged to *try completely new ways* of using movement creatively. Everyone is pioneering in this field and we need to share our ideas and experiments.

It is not necessary for the leader to have had dance training, but he will find value in summer courses in the field of dramatic movement and in creative dramatics. Basically the leader needs both enjoyment of children and excitement about living—personal interrelation and religious insight with a background of current religious, social, and psychological ideas.

Tips for Teachers

Pat Sonen in *Using Movement Creatively in Religious Education* gives these "Tips for Teachers":

Be adventurous.
Offer children a challenge.
Do not be disappointed too soon.
Do not use the negative approach and do not criticize.
Move with your children, in their way and in your own.
Help the children to keep experimenting.
Let the children see that you use their ideas.
Let the children be themselves.
Encourage, but do not insist or be directive.
Plan a quiet period to follow an active one.
Observe movement and become aware.
Develop the children's sensitivity to movement.

Your attitude counts! Remember, you are asking the children to do a natural thing; to move according to their bodies and their spirits. You are encouraging them to become involved in an expressive, healthy act. You are leading them to new awareness of senses and spirit; more pleasure in having, knowing, and using life.

No Set Procedure

Although some points have been itemized on pages 10-11, there is no set procedure. The leader must be sensitive to what the children are developing and encourage them to build on their own movement ideas; so one cannot proceed in any set way. The children and their ideas take priority; the leader has his importance as evaluator and encourager. The leader does not demonstrate, but may join in. He does not impose, but may expose and assist in involvement by contributing some fragments of ideas when there is a need.

When starting with a new group, sometimes it is effective to join in spontaneously with the children as one leader discovered when she did this:

The boys and girls thought this very funny indeed (and frankly we both felt a bit self-conscious and hoped that no one would look into the classroom just at that moment). On this particular occasion and on succeeding days we did get the children to join in with somewhat more enthusiasm, although it was obvious that most of them were imitating our movements. This was not exactly desirable, I felt, but this imitation at first might serve the purpose of helping the youngsters become less inhibited. Above all, it seemed to me of greatest importance that the children were gradually beginning to show enjoyment; in time they would become less imitative and more creative in their movements. At this point I learned . . . the teacher can help stimulate the children by *her own active participation,* by *her enthusiasm,* and by *her adventurous attitude.*

THE CREATIVE TEACHER

A leader in the field of creative dramatics, Grace Stanistreet, offers many keen insights in considering "Who Is a Creative Teacher?" Here are a few of her discoveries:

> *What the teacher is, grows from what he believes.* His whole being is a statement of his conviction, or his lack of conviction. . . . There is belief and respect for him who believes and respects. . . .
>
> Through his own growth, understanding, and observation, he sees that children are persons equal to himself and thus worthy of respect. . . . Creative teaching begins with a personal belief in children, and an expectation that the faith will be supported. Creative teaching begins with seeing children in the right perspective—not as exquisite, angelic cherubs, not as brats, but as human beings. . . . When each is accepted as a human being, there is a realistic relationship between teacher and child. . . .
>
> He [the creative teacher] thinks of teaching as helping the individual to use himself . . . by creating in him the desire for new knowledge and the desire to use it, by providing the chance for personal discovery and exploration. . . .
>
> The teacher creates a climate which lets the individual be himself. . . . The teacher creates opportunities for the individual to see himself whole, to see his true relationship to the world about him.

Be creative in the use of movement so that the child may make discoveries. Some discoveries come through experimenting, then making an intuitive leap toward an assumption that will require more investigating. Some discoveries come, not through seeking, but through being aware and thus seeing into something that might have been overlooked. So, discovery comes partly by searching and partly by not searching. And we discover that religious growth comes partly through seeking God's will and partly through not seeking, but just knowing that God's will is clear if we are aware.

Here we start both with anticipation and with humility to discover with children so that we may all grow in both discipline and awareness. "Time for discovery" is not just a special time in a church school; time for discovery is every moment of existence.

PART ONE

Creative Dramatic Movement
with Eight- and Nine-year-olds

Why use only your speaking voice and clapping hands to interpret thoughts and feelings when you have a whole body which may be used as an instrument of expression? . . . Movements seem to come from deep inside each boy and girl. No stereotyped set of motions. Each individual is expressing his own response to the Creator of earth and sky and sea. . . . Only the unimaginative ever could suppose that living could become so stern and solemn that no place would be left for "tuning in" with the rhythm of God's universe!

—LADONNA BOGARDUS

Eight- and nine-year-olds are restless and need movement. They are becoming aware of their environment and need creative and active ways to drain off frustrations, to adjust to new perspectives, and to recover their balance over and over again. Movement is one of their prime methods of readjusting themselves to their environment.

The child in this age-group wants to discover—to discover himself, to discover for himself about life that affects him, and to discover in his own way. There is no "right way" to discover; there are as many ways as there are children participating.

Eight- and nine-year-olds are full of cross currents of feelings and interests. They want to be involved in group activities and yet each one wants to be individually independent!

Leaders of such a group must be resilient, balanced, patient, adaptable and endowed with a healthy sense of humor. The word leaders (plural) is used, for in this age-group with such a wide range of interests and maturity an assistant is needed to work with an individual child or with a small group while the larger group is moving along together. This is no time for leaders to look for results, but it is a time to accept and to enjoy the discoverers and their discoveries.

1

DISCOVERING VARIETIES OF DRAMATIC MOVEMENT

HOW WE MOVE

Have you ever thought about all the "hinges" that connect the bones in our body? Hinges everywhere—from our heads down to our toes—hinges so that we can bend forward and back to the side and around! Let's try bending and using our hinges. . . . Some are little hinges and some are big hinges. . . . We can go forward and back, to the side and around. . . .

Where is the highest hinge in our body?

"The hinges in our neck?"

No, there's a higher hinge than that.

"My jaw?"

Yes, our jaw is very important as a hinge. Try talking without that hinge. . . .

"Our jaws are necessary for eating too."

Yes, it would be impossible to eat an ear of corn without good jaw hinges!

Now we'll go down our neck hinges . . . out our arms . . . to our fingers full of hinges . . . back up by our elbow hinge to our shoulders to our spine . . . down the spine hinges to our hips . . . down our legs to our toe hinges. . . . Some hinges go forward and back; some go only one way. Why? Our bodies didn't just happen. Everything has been planned or developed so that our body can do many things. . . . Our body is a wonderful gift that we should take care of to keep it strong and adjustable. And we must respect the bodies of other people and see that we don't hurt them.

A Negro folksong that children enjoy interpreting as they get acquainted with bones and hinges in their bodies is "Dry Bones" (from Ezekiel 37:1-10) which lists the various bones attached to each other, going from head to toes and from toes to head, in order that the people can stand and "hear the word of the Lord."

Since all parts of the body are discussed and all are related, the children will be interested in knowing that Paul referred to people in the church as parts of the body (1 Corinthians 12:14-31). Each one in the group is different and may do different things, but everyone is related and no one is better than another.

HOW WE BEND AND STRETCH

How small can each of us get? Curl up like a kitten into a ball of fur or like an astronaut in a small capsule. . . .

How tall can we get? Our arms are reaching up so high! Now we'll let our arms down and let our shoulders rest, but think of stretching through the top of our head. Feel like Alice in Wonderland when her neck grew longer and longer; her head got higher and higher!

How wide can we stretch? Our legs . . . our arms. . . . We need lots of room to spread out.

• • •

Some of the children's songs can be used for bending and stretching: "Planting Rice" can be sung while bending and swaying; "High Is the Blue Sky"* can be sung with arms up-stretched while walking.

Encourage the children to think of a creature or object that bends or stretches; then let them spend some time experimenting with the way it would feel to move like it. Allow a sharing time for each one to show what he is doing; see if the others can discover what he is acting out. There are endless possibilities: rubber band, jack-in-the-box, accordion, dredger, giraffe, waking up, octopus, hood of a convertible.

If the children have never experimented in this way, each child may be given a slip of paper with some suggestion for movement. Each child then moves like the object, but does not speak. This is similar to the game "Who (or What) Am I?" It is best, however, for each child to think up his own ideas.

FIGURE 1

HOW WE RUN

To run is more natural for a child than to walk, so a child enjoys discovering more about running. To run well one needs to get his weight forward, on the balls of his feet, and to breathe deeply (Figure 1).

• • •

Do you know how to run without getting out of breath? Let's run around our room, all in one direction but as fast or slowly as we wish. (*Everyone runs lightly. There may be music, clapping, or percussion. When the accompaniment stops, the children stand still. Quite a few are breathing heavily.*)

This time I want you to experiment with me. Before we run, try this first: breathe in while I count 1-2-3-4, and then out. Here we

go: in-2-3-4, out-2-3-4, in-2-3-4, out-2-3-4. Good! Now clap with your hands held up as high as your face while you breathe in during four claps; then clap with your hands held opposite your chest as you breathe out during four claps. Try it with me. (*Everyone claps four times, inhaling, diaphragm up with hands elevated; then exhales during four claps with hands lowered.*) Fine! You have the idea.

Now, as you run around the room, you don't need to clap, but just remember to breathe in as you take four running steps; then breathe out during the next four running steps. I'll remind you by calling out "in-2-3-4, out-2-3-4." We'll do this about ten times.

Here we go: in-2-3-4, out-2-3-4. . . . (*They all run evenly to the counts.*) Now, let's stop! Stand very still. . . . Why, you are all breathing easily. That really helped, didn't it? Why do you suppose it helped?

"Maybe I'm afraid that someone will catch me, so I hold my breath."

---

* These songs are in *The Whole World Singing*, compiled by Edith Lovell Thomas, pp. 22 and 76. "Planting Rice" is also in *Sing a Tune*, p. 66; Co-operative Recreation Service, Delaware, Ohio.

Yes, you forget to breathe out, don't you?

"We need to breathe out our old air so then we can breathe in some fresh air."

Well, let's sit down for a minute. In the Bible, in the book of Isaiah, we read about people who ran and did not get tired. Although correct breathing is a great help in not getting tired, there is a power that gives us even more energy. There is a divine energy in each one of us. When we know that God needs our energy—for something to be done—we find we have a tremendous energy beyond just our own!

I'll read a little here in the Bible: "Even youths shall faint and be weary, and young men shall fall exhausted; but they who wait for the Lord shall renew their strength, . . . they shall run and not be weary" (Isa. 40:30-31). You see, people who care about God are apt to have more energy.

This reminds me of a story of a boy in the South. He was running a very important race in a high school track meet. As he went running around the race track, some people saw his lips move. He won the race, and afterward someone asked him if he was saying something as he ran. His answer was, "I was trying to keep my legs from getting tired, so I would say, 'O Lord, you pick 'em up, and I'll put 'em down.'" That was like a prayer for more energy, wasn't it?

HOW WE TURN

There are many ways to turn. Let the children experiment with different ways. Sometimes the use of imagination as to the way they turn will spur them on to more variety and creativity. How does one turn when one is angry and leaving? . . . when one hears one's name called? . . . when one is hunting for a path? . . . when watching an airplane? . . . when riding a bicycle? Or how do certain things turn: top,

windmill, amusement park whirling carts, radar scanners, floodlight beams at an airport, floor-polishing brushes, tornado, nebulae, planets? It seems as if everything imaginable turns! And each thing turns in a unique way. The guessing game of "What Turning Thing Am I?" could be played for a while. This is a time for movement exploration.

Perhaps there will be a natural link to the turning of radar scanners, telescopes, nebulae, planets,° or the turning of the earth. Of course you can have some pictures of these on the bulletin board in the room and a child might notice one of them.

•   •   •

We are all interested in the turning of our earth, in the circling of the planets, and in the masses of stars that form swirling nebulae. (Show pictures.)

Let's be like swirling spiral nebulae, with stars way out on our fingertips (Figure 2). Swirl high and down and around, up high and down and around. . . .

Let's sit down for a minute and look at this picture of a huge radar telescope that is able to catch the tones and sounds from many stars. We can't hear these sounds with our ears, but there may be some space "music of the spheres." Do you know what a sphere is? It is a shape like a ball, like a globe—like the globe of the earth at school. A sphere may refer to a planet which is like our earth.

We are living on a planet—our earth—which is moving and turning as it goes on its special pathway through the sky. I wonder if our planet makes some musical tone as it travels along through space?

Do you know the song "This Is My Father's World"? It mentions this idea:

° Filmstrip Number 5 in the series "Creative Dramatic Movement," listed on page 74, shows eight- and nine-year-olds as planets.

19

All nature sings, and round me rings,
The music of the spheres.

• • •

The following excerpt from an article by astronomer J. Hugh Pruett may be useful:

Many of the ancient peoples believed that harmonious sounds were actually present in the starry heavens. Some worked out definite relations between the movements of the planets and their music. From this we get the expression "the music of the spheres."

The famous Grecian Pythagoras (sixth century B.C.) taught that as the planets swing through the firmament, they emit clear and pure musical notes. Since each note depended upon the planet's speed—and this in turn upon its distance—he felt that the spacing of these heavenly bodies was perfectly arranged, for the combination of the notes produced splendid harmony; indeed, a symphony so majestic as well-nigh to surpass human comprehension.

Shakespeare, in *The Merchant of Venice*, says:

There's not the smallest orb which thou behold'st,
But in his motion like an angel sings.

The library can furnish you with material on radar telescopes which pick up a variety of tones from planets and stars.

Interpreting Our Solar System

Here are some pictures of our special group of planets that revolve in our solar system—planets that move around our sun. . . . This dotted line indicates that this planet moves in this orbit or pathway, through space year after year.

Let's sit very still for a moment and think of the vast universe, while we listen to some of the music that Gustave Holst composed to sound like planets. *(Play recording of the beginning of "Saturn" in* The Planets.*)* The

———
*Albums are available from most record dealers.

FIGURE 2

space of the universe is so vast, . . . we can't even imagine how vast. . . .

We might act out the movement of the planets around the sun. I have nine round cards here with the name of a planet on each. As I give one to you, please fasten it on your shirt or your dress with the pin that is stuck on it. *(The children could have cut out, named, and numbered these planet disks.)* This big disk is for the sun which will be in the center, and then the planets will be in their special order according to their distance from the sun. When everyone is in order each planet will move to the right around the sun, for all the planets are moving and turning in the same direction. *(Start the music again.)*

Diane, will you take your place as the Sun in the center. . . . Closest to the Sun is Mercury. . . . Larry, you are Mercury. . . . In the next orbit is Venus. Yes—Sally. . . . And now comes the Earth. George. . . . Then comes

20

FIGURE 4

FIGURE 3

Mars . . . Jupiter . . . Saturn . . . Uranus . . . Neptune. . . . Finally we come to Pluto, way out on the farthest edge. (*Arms are held in wide arc, sometimes high and sometimes low as in Figures 3 and 4.*)

The Planets music seems to tell us that these planets are all moving, so here we go in our orbits, steadily turning, never stopping, . . . year after year . . . for thousands of years in the past and for thousands of years in the future. . . . Diane, as the Sun, you can be shooting out fire fountains as you turn, but turn very slowly, for you have a long job of turning. . . . Each of you can make a humming sound for your planet. . . . (*The children always hum when this is done out of doors where no music is played. . . . When you sense*

that the children have reached their maximum involvement in this design of movement, dim the music and then stop it and the children will stop.)

Let's sit down for a minute. How did you enjoy being a planet?

"I got tired. I'm glad I'm *not* a planet."

"The music was scary."

"I'd rather be an astronaut than a planet."

Astronauts are learning to plan their flights because our universe isn't just moving by chance. Scientists and astronauts will find out more and more but I doubt if they will find out everything, because God, who has planned the universe, guides and plans beyond any human understanding. God's power is always with us here or anywhere in the universe.

Here is a new hymn to sing. I have written the words for you to read first; then we might sing it.

21

THEY BLAZE A PATHWAY TO THE MOON

VICTORIA SAFFELLE JOHNSON

WIRTEMBERG

1. They blaze a path-way to the moon, The he-roes of the hour.
2. God sees them go; He goes with them, His thoughts in ev-ery mind,

They make the out-er dark-ness feel Man's grow-ing, might-y power.
His at-oms ev-ery-where, His light, His breath in all man-kind.

They move through God's e-nor-mous home Of stars and worlds and space,
How could we go a-way from God? To Him no place is far,

A-way be-yond this earth we know And still with-in His grace.
For God, who made this world of ours, Made all the worlds that are.

Let's rest a bit. Curl into a ball; put your head on your knees and wrap your arms around your legs. . . . Each one of us is like a planet. But planets can't choose to change their orbits. As human beings we can choose our paths and make new designs. Each one of us is a wonderful creation planned and made by God. Sometimes we call God "Father" because we know that God has planned for us and cares about us.

"This Is My Father's World"

I'm sure many of you have sung this song. Let's sing it (words on chalkboard):

> This is my Father's world,
> And to my listening ears,
> All nature sings, and round me rings
> The music of the spheres.
>
> This is my Father's world:
> I rest me in the thought
> Of rocks and trees, of skies and seas;
> His hand the wonders wrought.

Now, let's see if we can express this song with movements.* (The children decide world means "the universe," so they make a circle and move to the right. They don't want to hold hands.)

What does "listening ears" mean? How does one listen best? By standing still. (Discourage any gesture to the ear. Get the thought of the line.)

"Round me rings the music of the spheres" —that would be movement like the planets turning. (All turn around at their own speeds.)

"This is my Father's world." (They repeat walking in a circle as they did on the first line.)

"I rest me in the thought"—what does that mean?

---

* Described in Filmstrip Number 5, listed on page 74.

"It might mean that I'm going to sit down and think."

"Or we could just stand still to think."

"Of rocks and trees, of skies and seas"— these words are like a group of pictures. Let's take one at a time and finger-paint them in space. Before we move, we must think of different kinds of rocks. Now, try finger-painting what you are thinking (round, jagged, cliff, and so on).

Let's think of some special kind of tree (pine, willow, twisted or gnarled). We can feel the branching of that tree using our whole body. Experiment to see how the tree might move if a big wind were blowing. Stretch, bend.

Think of the wonders of the skies—clouds, stars, rainbow.

Now, seas—lakes, rivers, waterfalls.

(The children decide to choose just one image to express, making a composite instead of a fast sequence of interpretations.) A good idea.

• • •

The sequence of these ideas can be expressed with a flow of movements—starting low with small rocks, merging into the wonder of the upward thrust of growing things, the stretch from earth to sky, the downward sweep of rivers into a lake.

It might be well to sing and interpret this song as far as the children have gone in their explorations—up to the last line.

• • •

"His hand the wonders wrought." (Discussing the line with the children will keep them from considering it too literally.) That is a rather hard line to understand. What are some of the wonders?

"Stars."

"Ocean."

Yes, there are many wonders—everywhere. When I sing "his hand the wonders wrought," I think of God's mind that planned all the wonders. We don't see a mind, but what one says and does grows out of what one thinks and plans in one's mind. The swirling universe, the growth of a tree from a seed—those things don't happen except from the mind of God.

I have heard of a letter addressed in this way:

Jane Crofut,
  the Crofut Farm,
    Grover's Corners,
      Sutton County,
        New Hampshire,
          United States of America,
            Continent of North America,
              Western Hemisphere,
                the Earth,
                  the Solar System,
                    the Universe,
                      the Mind of God.

We can read that address the way it is written, and we can read it starting from the bottom address. That is the way mailmen in a post office sort out mail: they start from the bottom. That is our full address—beginning from the Mind of God!

(After some discussion, the children experiment to see how to express this sense of wonder in some all-inclusive and infinite way. Some look up first, reach up, then lower the arms thinking of the world about them and the earth where they live; others start to lift their arms very slowly and end holding them high, looking up; others turn in place as an all-inclusive gesture and then end with an upward reach.)

• • •

If the class is large, it can be divided into units of eight or ten, and each group can work out its own interpretations. Then they will enjoy showing their designs to each other. If evaluations are made, they should be in regard to *what expressed the meaning well* and whether *the main idea was expressed* (in con-

trast to just word pantomiming). For example, in the last line, just a simple lift of wonder is enough.

Interpreting a Poem

Sometimes the choral reading of a poem and dramatic action may be combined. Certain children enjoy moving more than reading and vice versa. The minimum amount of movement described below is just a suggestion; the group should work out their own ideas:

(Children step out occasionally to interpret ideas; then return to reading group.)
DIVISION 1:
Some things there are which make me know
That God is gentleness and power:
BOYS: Titanic Gothic peaks of snow—
(One or two boys step out from group and stretch up as peaks.)
GIRL: And—a white Alpine flower.
(One girl steps out in a low gesture.)
DIVISION 2:
Some things there are which make me see
That God is beauty, goodness, grace:
GIRLS: The growing greatness of a tree
BOY: Standing in some desert place.
(One child starts to extend arms as a branching, angular tree.)
DIVISION 1:
Some things there are which make me sure
That God is truthful, just, and pure:
DIVISION 2:
It is to watch his white stars swing,
And hear his choral planets sing.
(Three or four children turn and move in a circle.)

HOW WE WALK

Do you know that each one of you has a special way of walking? I know a person who is almost blind, but he can still see the general

24

FIGURE 5

outline shape of a person. He says, "I get to know who a person is by watching the way he walks." We tend to recognize our friends by looking at their faces, but our ways of walking are just as definite and different as our faces.

We also make little changes in the way we walk if we are in certain moods: really happy, excited, discouraged, scared, cross. Walking isn't just a matter of putting one foot before the other; your walking involves where you are looking, the way you hold your head, your shoulders, your elbows, your hands. These are all clues that show the mood you feel.

Let's see if we can guess just what mood each one of you is feeling. One at a time, walk across the room and back again, and then we will see if we have been able to catch the mood. Think first. The mood must be *real* to you. . . . We have some very good actors here. Good actors don't need to talk all the time; people catch the moods of actors by the way they move.

Interpreting a Parable

Jesus told a story about people who were walking on the road from Jerusalem to Jericho. It is the story of the good Samaritan.°

° Filmstrip Number 4, listed on page 74, shows eight- and nine-year-olds interpreting the story of the good Samaritan.

(Tell or read the story in Luke 10:25-37.)

If we want to put this story into an action-play we must get acquainted with all of the people. Who would be seen first on that road from Jerusalem to Jericho? The robbers? How do you suppose robbers feel as they hide, run, look back, crouch? Will you five run like robbers? . . . What a terrible way to live—always ready to run and hide because one knows he is doing wrong! This time I would like five others to run about eight steps and then stop to check up to see if anyone is coming. The rest of us can clap eight fast claps and wait; then do it again as we see the robbers run eight steps.

• • •

It is best to start with robbers since this action has great interest for this age. Let small groups take turns experimenting. If a large group runs at one time, there might be bedlam. A small group can decide how long to run before stopping to check. Then the observers become the percussion group to assist in clapping and they feel closely related to those in action. Often the clapping follows the pattern of 1-2-3-4, 1-2-3-4, hold, 1-2-3-4, 1-2-3-4, hold (eight claps in a unit; the "hold" is equal to a count of four).

• • •

The robbers see someone coming on the road (Figure 5)! Who would that be? . . . Yes, the tired traveler. Have you ever been on a long hike and been so tired and thirsty that you haven't even bothered to look around, but just watched the trail as you went step by step? Let's see what a tired way of walking you four can show. . . . Oh, what heavy boots! . . . Look at the arms dangling! . . . You know how to be tired all the way through. The rest of us can feel this with you by lifting one hand and letting it fall on our lap with a thud just as you thud along in your walking. Then the other hand. . . .

• • •

After a group has moved as tired hikers, one is chosen for the action and everyone else joins in with the percussion accompaniment. The thud is made by lifting a hand shoulder high and letting it drop onto the thigh; hands are alternated. The children follow the tempo of the traveler and so feel a part of each step he takes.

• • •

You remember in the story how the robbers sprang at the tired traveler, stole his purse and his cloak, and hit him so that he fell down among the rocks by the side of the road. Later, after we have discovered just how each person walked, we'll put the whole play together. Now the robbers have run away to hide for they see someone coming down the road. Do you remember who the first one was who passed by? . . . It was a priest.

A priest in those days long ago was one who had to follow many laws to keep himself clean. If he should touch some blood from a wound, it would take him a long time to get "purified" again. I think Jesus told this story because he wanted people to realize that the important thing is to help when there is need and not to think that "keeping certain rules" is the most important.

Let's imagine how it feels to walk like that priest—all closed in by rules. . . . This time I am going to ask David to lie down as the wounded traveler and I am going to ask Joan, Kevin, and Susan to take turns coming in, and walking by the traveler. . . . No one knows exactly how the priest walked so you can walk any way you wish. . . . (*Joan walks fairly near and pulls her skirt away. Kevin sees the traveler and walks in a wide arc away from him. Susan sees him, stops for a minute, and goes on.*) Yes, he could have acted in any of those ways. I am going to ask Susan to walk alone this time. Susan walked with small steps and she looked as if she were wrapped around with rules. Let's make a closed-in, muffled clap by holding our hands cupped a little. Clap for each of her steps and stop if she stands still. . . . Very good!

There is another passerby besides the priest. Do you remember what he was called? . . . A Levite. He was like a very busy lawyer—in a hurry. (*Several demonstrate, rushing about.*) Sometimes when we are in a hurry, our jaw is tight, our hands clenched; we look very tense and brittle. Let's have Gordon be the Levite and we can snap our fingers for each step he takes.

This time I will ask Kevin to lie down as the wounded traveler. Let's see what the Levite does. Are you ready to follow Gordon's pace with the snapping of your fingers? . . . (*Gordon walks fast, seems almost to trip over Kevin as he dashes on his way.*)

Why do you suppose the Levite didn't stop? "He might have been late to a meeting."

"Maybe he was going to report the accident to the police."

"Maybe he was scared that he might get hurt by robbers."

Kevin: "I stuck my foot out because I felt like tripping him, if he wasn't going to help me."

Well, now it is time for the Samaritan. He's a good hiker and is like a boy scout. . . . Let's see the best walk you can show us. Yes, swing your arms, . . . chest high, head up, and breathe out as well as in—just as you did when running. . . . What happened when he saw the wounded traveler? . . . He helped him. He bandaged his wounds and maybe gave him something to eat or drink. Then he helped get him to an inn.

Do you know how to help a person get up? Alan will show us. Alan, you may choose someone to help. . . . See how Alan gets John's arm over his shoulders. Now you can help him to walk. The good Samaritan brings him to the inn and even pays the innkeeper. After that, the good Samaritan goes on his way. Let's clap for his walk as if we were clashing cymbals.

This story was told a long time ago, but we still need to hear it because even today in the school yard, or at home or on a bus there are people who are mean, people who go right by, and people who really help.

Now let's put it all together. We have the five robbers who are hiding. David is ready at the far end. Behind him is Susan as the priest, behind her is Gordon as the Levite, and behind him is Alan as the Samaritan, and over at the other side is Joan as the innkeeper. All of the rest of us will make the right clapping sounds for all of you. David, here is a purse and a bag of food for the robbers to grab. Now we are ready. (*Everyone is involved in the sequence. The robbers agree that there will be three clapping units—eight in a unit—before they see the* traveler. *They decide where the traveler will be when they jump out of their hiding places. They have three clapping units before they see the priest and run to hide. . . . After the Samaritan leaves the inn, everyone ends with the swinging claps that are his walking accompaniment.)*

• • •

The children should have a chance to try most of the parts. Sometimes children need to drain off a mood by being robbers; sometimes a shy child needs to be encouraged to walk freely as the Samaritan. Allow time for discussion to see what new insights the children are getting, for they have been actively experiencing a story.

Interpreting a Psalm

Psalm 150 is full of action and music. Children of this age can study pictures of early Hebrew processionals and of the musical instruments that were carried in these processionals. Sometimes the junior highs will help them to make these instruments out of plywood by using a jigsaw to cut long slender trumpets (Figure 6), disks for cymbals (Figure 7), and semicircular, lyre-like harps (Figure 8). The children can string the harps with cord or twine and gild them with spray gilt. Four of each instrument could be made so that quite a few of the boys can lead the procession with them.

César Franck has written a dramatic arrangement for Psalm 150 which could be sung by a high school or adult choir and tape-recorded for the accompaniment of the children's processional. The children can clap the beat and then walk with a joyous and expectant stride.

The following part of Franck's anthem is used for the processional:

O, praise ye the Lord, praise God in the temple,

O, praise ye the Lord, in the firmament of his power,

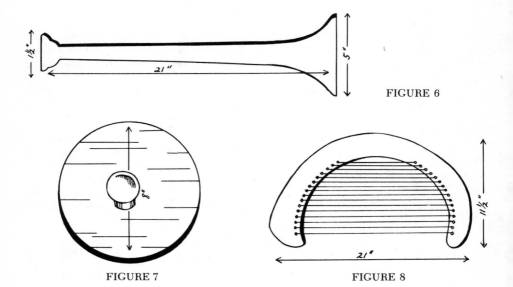

FIGURE 6

FIGURE 7

FIGURE 8

O, praise him for his might and the greatness of his wonders,
O, praise him, O, praise him, according to his majesty.

As the children walk to the steady beat, encourage them to feel like the Hebrew people entering the temple with praise to God for all the wonders of earth and sky. Perhaps there could be a worship center with a large spatter painting that suggests the wonders of earth and sky. This psalm can be related to the children's previous experience with the wonder of the universe. Their walking can be related to their earlier experience of walking as the good Samaritan.

Following the processional part of the anthem is a section on the musical instruments:

Praise the Lord, praise the Lord with the sound of the trumpet,
Praise the Lord, praise the Lord.
Praise the Lord, praise the Lord with the lute and the harp,

Praise the Lord, praise the Lord.
Praise the Lord with the timbrel, the timbrel and the dance,
Alleluia, Alleluia, Alleluia, Alleluia.

Some of the children will have suggestions of musical instruments or they can all imagine that they have a special musical instrument. Encourage the children to lift the trumpet high, to hold the harp up, to clash the cymbals or timbrels high. These musical instruments are used to express joyous praise.

In an account of working with a group of third-graders in a church school, Jean Beckwith Miller described how the children tried to understand the mood or idea of each section of Psalm 100. They experimented with ways to communicate this idea or mood. When they were considering "Make a joyful noise," one boy said, "I was going to skip, but you can't do that in a church." In recalling the comment, Jean wrote: "This I thought was very revealing. A child in our modern Western church

28

feels forbidden to express joy in his way!" Perhaps during the line "Praise the Lord with the timbrel, the timbrel and the dance," some of the children in your group could skip or leap. In the reference to David's dancing with all his might before the Lord, the word dance was closely related to exultant leaps.

During the last four alleluias, encourage the girls to turn and turn and reach up with wonder. Their experience as swirling nebulae will assist them here, but of course this will involve more variation and also a mood of exultation.

So the first section could be a processional led by those who have musical instruments. At the start of the second section, the ones with the musical instruments could have special actions:

Praise the Lord, praise the Lord with the sound of the trumpet: The trumpeters, with trumpets held high, cross past each other to opposite sides, and then turn about on "Praise the Lord, praise the Lord."

Praise the Lord, praise the Lord with the lute and the harp: Those with harps pass each other to opposite sides, and turn on "Praise the Lord, praise the Lord."

Praise the Lord with the timbrel, the timbrel and the dance: Those with timbrels or cymbals can cross with skips or leaps.

Alleluia, Alleluia, Alleluia, Alleluia: A group of girls can turn freely, feeling the emphases of the four alleluias.

These are suggestions, not directions. Each time one works with a group, there are variations and new ideas, and children of this age enjoy interpreting this psalm in their own ways.

If they are trying to recapture some of the Hebrew emphasis, the girls may enjoy having a flowing headdress, which can be stabilized in the hair by a small side comb sewn to the top center of the light scarf or shawl; the boys may accept a striped, sleeveless cloak such as the Arabs wear. The children can wear their own clothes basically. There is no point in going into total costuming, but some little suggestion of a costume often makes the children feel more like the Hebrew people.

HOW WE FALL

Usually if we fall down, it is a surprise to us! Let's pretend that all of you are rocks on the top of a wall of rocks. You are a row of top rocks. Perhaps you have seen stone walls. Early settlers cleared fields to plant crops and so they stacked the rocks and stones that they found in their fields and made stone walls along the edge of their property. Every once in a while the rocks would get loose and fall.

Can you imagine how some of those rocks might have fallen? Now, before you fall, I want to caution you, for the floor is very hard. Some rocks fall into grass or piles of leaves, but you will land on the floor. So don't land suddenly on the base of your spine, for you might injure a vertebra—one of the small bones in your backbone. Fall a little to one side and then roll out on the floor. Don't fall straight forward or straight backward. Bend some of those "hinges"; curve your body to break a stiff fall. Don't be too close to each other.

Now, let's see different kinds of falls. . . . *(They experiment. You may notice several unusual experiments and ask the children to show these to the others. Some roll or turn; some give several jumps before coming to a complete stop; some rock back and forth before falling.)*   •   •   •

Encourage each one to be different, to use imagination. You may tell the children that you will go behind the "wall" and each "rock" is to wait until you tap the "rock." The rocks that fall early are to lie very still until all the rocks have been tapped and have fallen.

FIGURE 9

Interpreting a Spiritual

Children are at different levels of maturity at this age. There are those who don't want to discuss; they just want to keep active. Sometimes it is good to let children use up extra physical energy by running and falling and thus find them ready for a quieter time. Following is a suggestion for "Joshua" which children enjoy dramatizing.* It is based on Joshua 6:1-6, 20. Perhaps it is best for use in vacation church schools or family camps where it may be done out of doors.

• • •

Do you know the story of Joshua and how his men were able to make the walls of the city of Jericho fall down, and so Joshua's men were able to capture the city?

* Filmstrip Number 4, listed on page 74, shows eight- and nine-year-olds interpreting "Joshua."

Have you ever noticed how vibration from music may make an object quiver or vibrate? Organ music has a lot of vibrations. Even playing a kazoo gives off vibrations that one can feel on one's lips. This story tells us that Joshua's men had trumpets and the vibrations from the sounds of those trumpets started to make cracks in the walls about that city. And before long the walls of stone fell down!

Let's learn a song about Joshua and then we'll use dramatic action with it:

Joshua fought the battle of Jericho, Jericho, Jericho,
Joshua fought the battle of Jericho
To make the walls come tumbling *down.*

(Repeat.)

(The last line has been changed because the walls should not fall down until the end of the third singing.)

30

Joshua fought the battle of *Jericho, Jericho,*
  Jericho,
Joshua fought the battle of *Jericho*
And the walls came tumbling down.

• • •

Half of the group will form the wall by making a circle facing out. Arms are raised shoulder-high, elbows bent, hands clasping neighbors' hands; elbows to forearms are close to neighbors' elbows and forearms. This gives the impression of a crenelated wall.

The other half of the group will be the trumpeters. They move around outside the circle-wall (Figure 9). They have imaginary or wooden trumpets (see Figure 6 on page 28) and move in clockwise direction with a light running step, making occasional lunges toward the wall on the syllables italicized in the stanzas above.

During the singing of the refrain the first time, the wall stands still and solid. As the same refrain is sung again, the tempo may be increased a bit, and the trumpeters become more active as they go about the wall. This time the stones in the wall begin to react by cracking and becoming unsteady as if some of the foundation stones are getting loose.

Finally, on the third stanza, the traditional words of the refrain are sung with increasing activity on the part of both groups. While they sing "and the walls came tumbling down," rocks come rolling down. The trumpeters step back and lift their trumpets high or reach up with a sense of victory.

2

DISCOVERING WAYS TO RELEASE TENSION

It is very hard to be eight or nine years old —younger children are "cuter" it seems for parents spoil them and take their side in quarrels; older children are "bossy" and have more privileges. If the eight-year-old is the oldest, parents are impatient, or they "put up" with his restless activity. These children are aware of the toughness of life in school. They have no perspective to help them ride out a sudden stormy situation. So these children are often in a state of tension, shown in increased activity and antisocial behavior. And all through the week the radio, TV, newspapers, magazines bombard them with the pressure of dangerous world conditions. Their comprehension is confused; they absorb a great deal of tension into their muscles and nervous system. They need some activities that release tension, so that they may be more resilient, and more able to meet tension.

Relaxation as a concept means nothing to the child of this age, so release from tension can be brought to him indirectly through (1) imagination and imagery, (2) humor, and (3) folk music and singing games with extrovert action.

Of course each child may not be helped by all of these approaches; the leader must try out various ways. The suggestions that follow are without any effect if the leader is full of tension. To be tense at times is natural, but sustained tension is destructive to bodily func-

tions and also a deterrent to reaching out creatively and openly. If we are going to *discover with* the children, we must feel open and expectant. Leaders might find clues for themselves in *Look Up and Live*,* written for adults.

RELEASE THROUGH IMAGINATION

Marionettes are like puppets except that marionettes have strings that hold them up. Let's be like marionettes with four strings that hold us up. One string holds our head up; one holds our hip up so that we can bend forward; then the last two strings are attached to our wrists. Let your arms feel light as if a string were holding them (Figure 10).

Now we are going to see what happens as we imagine that one of the strings is snipped. Here we go: One of your wrist strings breaks! . . . Down falls that limp arm. *(It swings like a pendulum that gradually comes to a still hanging.)* The other wrist string breaks! . . . Now the head string! . . . *(Each dangles forward and gradually comes to hang in a motionless state.)* Last of all, the hip string! . . . And there are all the marionettes lying on the floor as limp as if they were rag dolls.

* *Look Up and Live* by Margaret Palmer Fisk (Taylor). The Sharing Company.

FIGURE 10

Imagination, with no movement, can assist in a relaxation period. The imagery suggestions may be added to or deleted according to what might be of interest to your group. Leave time between the quietly spoken suggestions, as indicated by ellipses. Sometimes soft music can be used. The children may lie on the floor, but if this is not possible, let them rest their heads on a table. Try to have space between the children.

• • •

You are lying on a little raft—a raft that is just the right size for you. The sun is very bright, so you shut your eyes. Your raft is a little way from the beach, just floating about . . . drifting over the water. . . . The water has little swells that lift your raft gently and then let your raft go down softly. . . . The sun is warm. . . . There are no clouds in the sky—just blue, blue sky. . . . Not far away there is a sea gull floating and swooping in the air. . . . . Now your raft is drifting slowly toward the beach. It turns a little . . . as the small waves lap against it. . . . Each little wave moves it closer to the shore. . . . Now it is shoving against the sand. . . . So we'll have to think about getting up. Stretch a little. . . . And now sit up—like a frog on a lily pad!

Well, how did you feel on your raft?

"My raft seemed to go around and around."

"I saw a sailboat."

"I wanted to go far out to sea."

• • •

If the children enjoy this relaxation through imagery, experiment with lying on the beach and being covered with heavy dry sand, or having climbed high up on a mountain, lean back to rest and continue with near and distant imagery.

Let's be marionettes again. Karen is going to call off which strings are to break. (*Karen faces the group.*)

"Snip goes the head string! (*All heads dangle forward and shoulders sag.*) Snip goes one arm. (*Everyone hangs by one wrist and a hip string.*) Snip goes the hip string. . . . Snip goes the arm string." (*Everyone is on the floor.*)

It feels good to lie on the floor after dangling so long. . . . How would you like to be a marionette and not be able to do things by yourself?

"I wouldn't like to be one *really*."

No, I'm sure we are glad to be ourselves. And now, Timmy, would you like to call the snips, for we have time to do it once more.

33

RELEASE THROUGH HUMOR

Do the children seem to be in a disgruntled mood or are they silly and giggly? There is no escape; you must start with them where they are. Anyway, they would just as soon shift into another mood, but of course they won't change by being given an order to do so.

• • •

Do you feel sometimes as if everything just lands on you? Crushes you, mashes you? . . . I guess everyone knows that feeling. Let's groan or growl. . . . What a noise! Let's do it again. You know, you can growl even louder if you take a deep breath and then you will have a lot of breath to make an enormous, long groan.* Ready? (There are such tremendous groans that everyone laughs.)

This time, when you groan again, can you make yourself look like one big groan—like clay being pushed into a lump? As you groan, just see what your body feels like doing. (There is a mass of groaning and writhing!)

Now the next thing after exhaling all your breath, is a full inhaling—breathing in—so you will need to give room for your lungs to expand. That means that we will stretch and reach out or up as we breathe in. Try anything that occurs to you as you breathe in—some real contrast to the groan movement. But we'll start with the groan, taking about four counts to breathe out as we groan, then four counts to breathe in as we stretch. Here we go: (Groan-2-3-4; stretch-2-3-4). Good!

Now that we are not crushed down anymore, we can laugh. How do we laugh with our hands and arms as well as our voices? . . . Try some laughs. . . . I heard some short little laughs and some heavy low ones. Do you realize that when you laugh you are breathing out?

---

* The process of changing moods (groan-stretch-laugh) is described and sketched for adults in *Look Up and Live*, pp. 72-81.

. . . Let's sprinkle some light laughs with four little ha-ha-ha-ha's; then let's swing some low laughs with four ho-ho-ho-ho's. They are slower and heavier. And we'll have to take a quick breath just before them. And another quick breath after them so that we can end with a loud "hi!" and a high swing of our arm. That "hi" is a surprise ending. When we do it we can turn suddenly toward someone as we say it. Let's try the four light ha-ha-ha-ha's with light gay movements, then four slower ho-ho-ho-ho's with bigger movements. Take a quick breath and swing into "hi." Here we go. . . .

(The children do not need to keep within this framework, but they get the idea of contrasts in breathing and in moods and movements.)

• • •

At one session, a child said, "Let's do the groan and then the laughs." As she said this she moved first in the crushed-down position, then stretched her arms to laugh. The author said, "I do hope you won't forget the middle part which is like a bridge from a groaning mood to a laughing mood. In that bridge you breathe in, stretch, and look up. If you forget that bridge, this is what happens: you groan . . . and then you laugh, but your laughter sounds hollow and screechy like the laugh of an old witch—he-he-he-he . . . haw-haw . . . hump. Horrible! You must let yourself be filled with fresh air and you must let yourself be lifted above your agony of crushed feelings. Only then is your laughter going to be free and without tension. And the 'hi' at the end means you are ready to get along with people again."

RELEASE THROUGH FOLK GAMES

Songs of pioneer times and gay folk dance music are a part of every child's heritage. There are many simple ones that can be done and do not need girl-boy partners. A gay folk dance is a good way to start a dramatic movement time. The children feel acquainted; the action is simple and the music releases the child because of its folk quality. Folk dances are especially good for vacation church schools and camps.

"Jennie Crack Corn"° is like a Virginia reel except that the children can sing the call "Right hand . . . both hands," . . . and so on, and also the recurring words "I don't care." What a joy to feel irresponsible for a while and sing out!

"Gustaf's Toast"° is a European folk dance, which is sung. It is very easy: forward and back; arches to skip under. The children of this age are not particularly interested in each other in the boy-girl relationship, but group participation of this sort lays a wholesome foundation for later boy-girl activities.

Besides immersing people in rhythmic extrovert music, folk dances provide therapy in that most of them involve general group action and then a section where one couple does a special leading part, so the individual has a period of personal recognition and yet feels completely a part of the whole group. Recreation can be re-creation when it brings joyous energetic release and wholesome group consciousness.

° These singing games are found in *Handy Play Party Book.* Copyright, 1940, by Lynn Rohrbough. Cooperative Recreation Service, Delaware, Ohio. "Jennie Crack Corn" is on page 22; "Gustaf's Toast," on page 116.

3

DISCOVERING WAYS TO INTERPRET CHRISTMAS CAROLS

DECK THE HALLS

The early meaning of "carol" was to move in a circle while singing. Carols were melodies that the folk of the village participated in, singing and circling—in other words, caroling.

There are references to the fact that "Deck the Halls"* was danced in England on the village greens, but there is no explanation of how it was danced, so the children can evolve some simple pattern of movement that has meaning for them. The leader may have some knowledge of English folk dances or American singing games and make suggestions from these.

Here are some ideas for a group design for the first stanza of "Deck the Halls," but it can be repeated for all of the stanzas. Feel free to adapt any of these designs and to create completely new designs. Although the term "joining hands" is used, the leader may find that it works out better to have the children hold wreaths. Small six-inch or eight-inch paper wreaths may be purchased—enough so that each child holds *his* wreath in his right hand. When the circle is to be joined, each child holds onto the wreath at his left (Figure 11). This contributes an acceptable "insulation" for children who do not want to hold hands. It is better to have several circles of eight or

* The use of this carol is described in Filmstrip Number 5, listed on page 74.

ten each than to have twenty or thirty in a single circle.

Deck the halls with boughs of holly: Circle with joined hands and move to the left with a light, springy step as in English country dances.

REFRAIN: During first half, go into center, hands joined and lifted; during the last half, go backward to original circle area.

'Tis the season to be jolly: Same pattern, only circling to the right.

REFRAIN: Same pattern as for the preceding refrain.

Don we now our gay apparel: Let go of hands; each one turns in place with light steps and holds one hand high as he turns (*or* with his wreath in his right hand, high).

REFRAIN: Join hands and repeat the pattern of the previous refrains.

Troll the ancient, yuletide carol: One couple, previously agreed upon, makes an arch; the opposite couple then leads toward this arch. As they go under the arch they separate and these two lead their respective lines around the outside of the circle and back to their starting place. After the last couple has gone under the arch, the couple that has formed the arch then turns under its own arch.

REFRAIN: Usually the first part of the refrain is needed for the return of the whole group from going under the arch. So during the last line the forward and back design may have

FIGURE 11

to be shortened to just the raising and lowering of the arms. Otherwise the refrain remains the same.

In the traditional English morris dances, the dancers usually wore bells. The children may enjoy wearing an elastic with a bell or bells on their ankles or wrists. Wearing them on their ankles encourages the children to make light, springy steps to bring out more jingles from their bells.

JOY TO THE WORLD

"Joy to the World" can be interpreted in many ways, but here is a description of a design that one group of nine-year-old children evolved. Remember, the pattern need not be followed, but it may provide some ideas.

STANZA ONE:

Joy to the world, the Lord is come: The group forms a circle with hands joined. Everyone circles to the left, heads held high, singing and smiling. All stop like an exclamation point (!) at the end of this thought, as "come" is sung. Everyone stands straight.

Let earth receive her King: The group circles to the right in the same mood of joy, stopping like an exclamation point as "King" is sung.

Let every heart prepare him room: Everyone swings his arms (still holding hands) forward and back as a rhythmic expression of happiness. (*The children chose this as being a natural, happy movement.*) Arms swing forward and back spontaneously in any timing, some faster, some slower.

37

And heaven and nature sing: Everyone stops holding hands, and swings his arms up vertically, looking straight up as he sings "and heaven"; then lowers his arms as he turns around in place once, while singing "and nature sings." He may turn to the right or left, either way he wishes. The turning symbolizes an all-inclusive feeling of the wonders of nature about him (something like the swirling nebulae).

And heaven and nature sing: The previous design is repeated, possibly with a turning in the opposite direction.

And heaven, and heaven: The arms swing straight up during the first "and heaven." During the second "and heaven" everyone stretches upward a little higher with increased wonder.

And nature sing: Everyone now lowers his arms with a feeling of quiet joy.

STANZA TWO:

He rules the world with truth and grace: Everyone circles to the left, heads held high with the assurance of God's supreme power.

And makes the nations prove: The group circles to the right in the same mood.

The glories of his righteousness: The children hold hands in the circle and swing arms forward and back, forward and back (just a "thinking rhythm").

And wonders of his love: Letting go of hands, everyone swings his arms up vertically on "and wonders," then turns, lowering arms while singing "of his love." The upward reach of wonder is balanced by the sense of God's love flowing down on all of his creation partly through the coming of Christ and partly through Christ's love flowing through each one in all the relationships about him.

And wonders of his love: The preceding design is repeated, possibly with a turning in the opposite direction.

And wonders, wonders: The arms swing up and everyone reaches up, and stretches a bit farther, sensing infinite wonder.

Of his love: Everyone lowers his arms with a feeling of reverence.

ANGELS WE HAVE HEARD ON HIGH

Although the angels referred to by name in the Bible happen to be masculine, in our day we tend to envision angels as feminine, possibly because of early Christian art in which angels appear with long skirts and flowing hair. (However, scrutinize the angels circling above the nativity scene by Botticelli, and you will see strong masculine faces!) But it might be hard to convince eight- and nine-year-old boys that they should be angels; so if angels are to be portrayed by children of grade school age, they should be portrayed by girls.

The beautiful carol "Angels We Have Heard on High," with its refrain of "Gloria in excelsis Deo," invites one to whirl around with a feeling of glory. The spiraling notes offer the child a musical pattern that she can express in spiraling turns. As they turn, the girls should learn to be aware of where they are in relation to others so that they fill the space freely, but without colliding with another.

As they sing "Gloria" some of the children may want to turn three times which is the general division of the musical phrasing; some may wish to drift and turn; others may feel like turning more than three times because they enjoy turning. The children may need to be reminded to hold their heads up and to look up during the high parts of their turns.

At the close of the refrain, during the singing of "in excelsis Deo" there may be a turning or coming into the center from wherever the children have been—a turning toward a high center. Praying hands are lifted during "in excelsis" (in the highest) and lowered to a

FIGURE 12

position of adoration during "Deo" (Figure 12). Sometimes the children like to kneel at this point or at the end of the repeated part of the refrain.

Here are some general suggestions for the first stanza:

Angels we have heard on high: The children gather from various parts of the room.

Sweetly singing o'er the plain: They improvise with floating turns and arms extended.

And the mountains in reply: Everyone raises one arm and looks up, possibly moving away from the center.

Echoing their joyous strain: A design similar to the one for line two is used, possibly in the opposite direction.

REFRAIN

STANZA TWO:

Come to Bethlehem and see: The children move toward the imaginary crèche in the center.

Him of whom the angels sing: They swirl out from the center, extending an arm, as if inviting others to come to adore.

Come, adore on bended knee: Everyone comes to the center and kneels with head bowed.

Christ our Lord, our newborn King: The arms may be lifted, widened, and brought to rest at sides, slightly extended—all with a sense of wonder.

REFRAIN

This carol will involve the previous learning of how to turn, with more variations than have been done for nebulae, and "Joy to the World."

As the children sing "Gloria" they may think of the uplifted "O" of their arms made wide and high. Then their arms break apart at the top as though the children are catching a glimpse of more glory. The arm movements of forming a high arch and of spreading apart are linked with spiral turns.

The children will need to practice kneeling so that they will have grace and control. If the forward foot is turned out there is more of a base; if the foot in the rear keeps the ball of the foot on the floor there is more control and more ease in rising quickly. When the children kneel they should not crunch down low unless there is some special reason to do so. Most of the time a straight kneel means that there could be a straight line from the knee that touches the ground up that thigh, up through the torso to the head. They should practice kneeling on each knee so that they can kneel equally well on either one. When they are portraying this carol and come to a place where they wish to kneel, they should feel free to kneel on whichever knee they choose.

In referring to Botticelli's "The Nativity" in

39

which the angels move in a circle above the Holy Family, Nathaniel Micklem writes:

What more natural thing than that in the early days of the church's history the faithful should join hands in the church below at the time of sacred worship and consciously join in the dance of the angels of heaven? Let us remember that poetry and music and the dance are nearer to revelation than is doctrinal statement. Our faith rests in God, not in the propositions of the theologians. . . . We may even venture the opinion that doctrinal statement divorced from music, song, and dance is dead.

Moving with meaningful expressions to carols, hymns, spirituals, and psalms helps children who are eight or nine years old to feel vitally connected with their church and what it is trying to communicate.

PART TWO

Creative Dramatic Movement with Ten- and Eleven-year-olds

Religion has suffered more from the lack of any dancing spirit of joy on the part of its friends than it has from the vicious attacks of its enemies. . . . By "dancing" I mean the feeling of spiritual joy which tells us that here is something too big and lively to permit us to be content with a sedate walk—a joy which needs some rhythm to mark it.

—THE CHRISTIAN CENTURY

Ten- and eleven-year-olds are eager to understand more about themselves as individuals and also to understand more about others around them, and they are intrigued with people of other races and nationalities. They are much more interested in working as a group than the younger ones.

Also at this time they are preadolescents who are in the stream of adolescent consciousness. They dream of themselves in a new way; they are becoming aware of their inner self. To gain a sense of assurance at this time will undergird them in their adolescent years. To sense God's power and God's acceptance of them as they live each day is the strong base for more complex understanding of life. To work together as a group—sharing discoveries, experimenting, grasping new insights—strengthens their sense of relatedness in the adventure of living. As they explore the use of dramatic and symbolic movement, they grow in these various areas.

"Christian learning involves participation in experiences that change the self, that illuminate and liberate the self," writes Roger Shinn in *The Educational Mission of Our Church*. It also involves encounter. He says, "Persons face each other, discover their . . . enmities," and learn acceptance. Creative dramatic movement assists such Christian learning because it involves the whole child—his thinking, feeling, acting, reacting, reaching out, searching into his own depth—both as an individual and as part of a group.

Ten- and eleven-year-old children are full of contradictions in their likes and dislikes, in their realism and in their fantasy, in their enjoyment of competition and in their need for isolation. They vary widely in their development so that dramatic movement must cover a variety of ideas and moods. In Part Two there will be individual discovery of movement and also experimenting with symbolic movement patterns as a group experience.

1

DISCOVERING DRAMATIC MOVEMENT

HOW SMALL MOVEMENTS MAY GROW INTO LARGE ONES

Writing Our Names in Space

How important our names are! They are much more than a word with a certain mixture of letters. Pretend that you are signing an autograph book. You can hold the palm of your hands as the open book and write your name on it with an imaginary pen. . . .

Now pretend that your finger is a piece of chalk and you have a good-sized chalkboard on which to write your name. . . . You'll need more space, so you might spread out a bit. . . . My, some of you used a huge chalkboard! Or perhaps you have very long names.

This time we will need even more space because we will use our whole self—our full height for the high loops, and bending way over (almost mopping the floor) to make the low loops. Feel the long flowing lines or the sharp peaks and don't forget to dot any "i." Let's have three at a time write their names and we'll see if we can follow what they are writing in space. . . .

• • •

If this is a new group, some children may get acquainted in this way.

Starting with a Small Movement

With a new group that may be self-conscious, it might be well to start with some small movement and let it expand. Have the children shut their eyes and start to move one isolated part of their body. Let it move in and out, back and forth, or rotate, over and over again, until a rhythmic pattern seems to take shape, and then see if other parts of the body become involved in an expanded swinging or rotating or in counterbalancing the extended movement. (For example, one might begin by moving a finger, then a hand, an arm, head, upper torso, full torso. If the movement starts with a back and forth motion, this may be increased to include the sequence of portions of the body as listed above. If the movement starts with rotation, the increase may be continued in that form.) Try different starting areas and then see what develops. Nothing is ever the same. After a feeling of full expansion, it is good to decrease gradually—returning to the original starting movement—and then wait in complete stillness. The body will be relaxed and this time of quietness will be welcomed.

This type of experimenting with creative movement allows freedom for the child to see what emerges; it also suggests the movement pattern of starting, reaching a climax, and reaching an ending.

Karen may have been reading about amoebas reaching out. If she mentions this idea as a small-to-large possibility, you could ask her to bring some drawings of amoebas. Winifred

FIGURE 13

FIGURE 14

Several of the children may experiment with reaching out into the unknown with a "protoplasmic paw" (Figure 13); then go on to experiment with the branching plant life moving in the flow of the ooze (Figure 14); then breaking away and moving as a free cluster of related cells. What expansion possibilities starting from an amoeba!

Peter may have spent some weeks by the ocean watching tides and surf. Encourage him to develop some movement of both knowledge (through science) and wonder (through mystery). Physicist Richard Feynman, with all his scientific knowledge, admits the wonder behind so many things in our world. He writes:

I stand at the seashore, alone, and start to think. There are the rushing waves . . . mountains of molecules, each stupidly minding its own business . . . trillions apart . . . yet forming white surf in unison. Ages on ages . . . before my eyes could see . . . year after year . . . thunderously pounding the shore as now. For whom, for what? Never at rest . . . tortured by energy . . . wasted prodigiously by the sun . . . poured into space. A mite makes the sea roar.

Deep in the sea, all molecules repeat the patterns of one another till complex new ones are formed. They make others like themselves . . . and a new dance starts. Growing in size and complexity . . . living things, masses of atoms . . . ; dancing a pattern ever more intricate.

Out of the cradle onto the dry land . . . here it is standing . . . atoms of consciousness . . . matter with curiosity. Stands at the sea . . . wonders at wondering . . . I . . . a universe of atoms . . . ; an atom in the universe.

Duncan has caught the dramatic movement in her "Amoeba Proteus":

Push the protoplasmic paw out into space,

. . . .

. . . bravely to finger the unknown
In all directions. . . .
Thus through the eons we trace you, magically mobile. . . .
We, the adventurers, in our own journey through space,
Salute you!

The same thrill, the same awe and mystery, come again and again, when we look at any problem deeply enough. With more knowledge comes deeper, more wonderful mystery, luring one on to penetrate deeper still. Never concerned that the answer may prove disappointing, but with pleasure and confidence we turn over each new stone to find unimagined strangeness.

There is a dynamic power in imagination that can aid in discovery. Imagination may assist in penetrating objective matter and assist by being the dynamic trigger for experimental dramatic movement. Imagination and scientific knowledge can be mutually invigorating. The Christian education teacher should be aware of what scientific material the child is absorbing in school and then build into this a deeper consideration with its further reach of wonder. Christianity says "Yes" to scientific discovery, but Christianity continues, saying: "There is a great mystery also and we keep discovering fragments of this—in our universe, in ourselves, and in our relation to others."

HOW WE STAND

Just as each of you has your own name and your own thoughts, so each of you has your own posture—your own way of standing. What you think and feel affects your posture—how you breathe, how you think of others, how you consider the meaningfulness of your existence —all these affect the way you hold your diaphragm, your shoulders, your head.

Good posture is the balanced arrangement of the parts of your body so that you allow an adequate and effortless way for your bones, muscles, lungs, and your nervous system to function. Every part of your body is involved in posture.

A certain amount of training and understanding is important in order to have good posture, but equally important is the inner sense of ability to get along with others in your environment, to get along in any situation that you may meet, and to accept uncertainty with resilient faith.

Douglas Campbell, psychiatrist, has written in an article titled "Posture: A Gesture Toward Life":

> If posture is a gesture toward life, our treatment of incorrect posture should lay more emphasis on the social factors in the personality. . . . What we are dealing with in cases of incorrect posture is not a disturbed effector system, but a disturbed personality. The effector system is expressing very vividly, as it is supposed to do, its owner's attitude toward the problems of existence. Change the attitude and you change the effector response. . . . Posture is [an individual's] adaptation; we observe how he "stands" in relation to the demands of life.

So to help a child achieve better posture we may give him some clues and use imagery, but the greatest help may come indirectly through his learning to feel "at home" with his own self, with others, and with the mysteries of existence.

Experimenting with Posture

Let's try on some bad posture—just like trying on some dumpy clothes. . . . That's the way: sunken chest—no way for the lungs to get enough air; head forward—the nerves in the neck are all crushed together; weight back on the heels—the muscles have to make an extra effort to get us moving.

Do you know that the atmosphere actually causes some pressure on top of you? Then when you get into a "jam"—forgetting to do some job or being scolded for something you hadn't meant to do—that adds to the pressure; so it's just as if a pile driver came pounding down on you. Take your fist and let it be like the hammer of a pile driver. Pound it a few times on the top of your head. . . . Your body gets in a zigzag alignment . . . worse and

FIGURE 15

worse. *(Everyone is in a slumped, hopeless, grotesque position.)*

Now let's try on some good . posture—pretending that we are trying on a trim ski suit. . . . That's it, your chest and head are higher and your shoulders are straight. That ski outfit looks very neat on you. If you had a carpenter's plumbline, the weight would go straight down from your chest to the top of the arch of your foot—not down the back of your heel (Figure 15). Skiers always have their weight forward a bit.

Now, if you take a few pile-driver poundings on the top of your head . . . the pounder just bounces right up again. You don't get mashed down, but you are as straight as a good nail being hit by a hammer—not bending

or crumpling down. The way you stand really is important.

Do you know that the way you think and feel influences the way you stand? Pretend that you are standing waiting for a parade to come down the street. A car with a loudspeaker comes by announcing that due to circumstances beyond control the parade will be delayed one hour. What does that do to your posture? Oh, that's very bad. The worst part of that bad posture is that you are going to get even more tired because your body is in bad alignment. . . . All of a sudden you notice people looking up the street, so you straighten to your full height—and what do you see! A helicopter skimming along close to the street's surface! You breathe in; you are standing straight and you don't even think of being tired!

Do you know that just the opposite is true too? The way you stand makes a difference in the way you feel. If you feel discouraged sometime, instead of going into a dismal slump, say to yourself, "OK, that's the way it is, but just the same, I'll hold my head up and stand straight." You take a deep breath and suddenly you'll find you have a new idea that will help you not to be as discouraged as you were. It really works! Did you see *The King and I?* When the mother and her six-year-old son are going to land in a strange country, the mother sings a song to her son: "Whenever I feel afraid, I hold my head erect and whistle a happy tune" and in the end she says she gets her own self convinced that she isn't afraid. She knew that secret too. Try it sometime, will you?

● ● ●

This might be too long as a standing session. Let the children sit down as they discuss. They may have dramatic illustrations of their own to share with the others.

● ● ●

46

Have you read the story in the Bible about a woman who was bent over? (Luke 13:11-13) Jesus noticed her and told her that she was free from whatever had seemed to keep her crushed down. He laid his hands upon her, and immediately she stood straight and praised God.

When Jesus spoke about taking his yoke (Matthew 11:28-30) he was talking to the people of his time who carried loads or burdens by placing a wooden yoke across their shoulders with a curve cut out to make room for the neck. Then the loads were fastened at the two projecting ends. Jesus knew how one had to stand straight to carry such loads, but he added that his yoke would rest easy and the burden wouldn't seem heavy. I think he might have meant that if we will bear burdens—busy with jobs that are helpful—we won't find them crushing us down.

Learning to improve our posture is a way of appreciating the gift of our amazing body and of seeing that our body is strong and in alignment if we are needed to carry heavy loads. And we might as well learn, for no one escapes carrying heavy loads. Even now many of you have some very heavy responsibilities, I know.

HOW WE EXPRESS DRAMATIC CONTRASTS

At first children may experiment in dramatizing an intense basic mood. Pat Sonen tells of a teacher's report on this:

When the class was expressing grief in movement, I was amazed to find one person whirling about the room covering his face with fingers and hands. His was a two-handed grief. Then another child covered the face with only one hand, and looked carefully where she was moving. I almost spoke out to another child for I couldn't see how what he was doing was really grief. He was on his knees, bent over with head on the floor, not moving a muscle. I caught myself in time. Who was I to tell him what grief was? Perhaps this is the way he would react to a sorrowful situation; just be still, and accept it. When I thought about it later, [I realized that I had] seen persons react in the same very quiet way to a sad accident.

But children find movement more dramatic when contrasts of moods are involved. So we need to discover ways to express these contrasts clearly. The basic contrast of movements lies between open, outward, advancing movement and closed, inward, withdrawal movement. Urge the children to consider contrast pairs: I am sad—but I can find something that makes me happy; examinations today—vacation tomorrow; I am scared—but I can be brave; questioning—answering. The children will think up their own contrasts.

"Nobody Knows the Trouble I've Seen"

In this spiritual we experience the contrasts of accepting trouble and surmounting trouble.° Let the children discover the contrasting moods and interpret them.

Nobody knows the trouble I've seen, nobody knows: Each one starts with some movement of discouragement, some movement that can be repeated.

But Jesus: Here is a quick contrast, a sudden idea: Jesus would understand!

Nobody knows the trouble I've seen: But there is the return to the original discouragement movement.

Glory hallelujah: Some upward, outward, forward, dynamic movement (Figure 16). "Hallelujah" is a Hebrew word that is hard to translate into English. It is something like a religious way of saying "hooray." One is like a cheerleader for God—accepting trouble and knowing that victory is possible.

° *In Look Up and Live* by Margaret Palmer Fisk (Taylor), pp. 53-71, this spiritual is described more fully and has illustrations for adults.

FIGURE 16

Sometimes I'm up, sometimes I'm down: Now comes the awareness of the times one is "up" and the times one is "down." These are fast contrasts. Children know how fast moods can change. So each child expresses this contrast.

Oh, yes, Lord: This is a time of acceptance. It is as if one said "OK." Of course no one likes trouble, but sometimes one grows more when one has to face troubles. When we say "Yes, Lord," we accept the possibility that God is expecting us to grow in the midst of troubles. What kind of a gesture could express this?

Sometimes I'm almost to the ground: Why not return to the movement that was used in "sometimes I'm down"—possibly a variation in angle or possibly lower.

Oh, yes, Lord: Why not repeat the acceptance movement—possibly with a different angle.

Then the whole refrain should be repeated, starting with "Nobody knows" but ending with "Glory hallelujah." Take a good deep breath before you sing or move to "Glory hallelujah." It will have to be a fast inhaling, but that really starts your change of mood from contracting to extending.

•   •   •

This Negro spiritual is valuable because of its deep contrasting feelings that are expressed so simply. In the fifth and sixth grades the child is on the threshold of the adolescent period. He is sensing the moods of exhilaration and of frustration, and right at this period he needs to see life with its contrasting moods in the encircling frame of a relationship to God (Creator and Sustainer) who understands him and helps him rise above crushing feelings.

In referring to ten- and eleven-year-olds, psychiatrists observe that developmental potentials come in paired opposites which are progressively woven into reciprocal balance. Recognition of "reciprocal balance"—of opposites that are understood and controlled, and of awareness that dualistic balancings are in all universal motions as well as human emotions— leads to gradual integration as the child grows into maturity. He gains clues to help him have poise, and these clues give him a resilience in meeting pressures and crises.

A more objective approach can be made in the dramatizing of "Nobody Knows." It can be linked to a study of the early way of picking cotton. The workers in the cotton fields dragged long bags into which they put the cotton that they picked from the low cotton plants growing in long rows. The Negro workers sang as they slowly trudged along picking the cotton, dragging the long bag (slung from the shoulder), bending over the low bushes,

48

but occasionally needing to straighten up, perhaps to stretch the arms while singing "Glory hallelujah."

The whole room can be a cotton field and everyone can feel the monotonous drudgery of cotton picking made more bearable by singing this spiritual which combines low rhythmic movement and occasional high movement rising into a release that gives renewal of strength. Boys may prefer this more objective approach especially if dramatic movement is new to them. Another time the more introspective and more creative approach may be presented. In experimenting with dramatic movement, the teacher must use his judgment as to the mood of the group.

"Ezekiel Saw the Wheel"

The ideas suggested here for "Ezekiel Saw the Wheel"• need not be followed, but are presented as a creative experiment with children of this age.

Perhaps Ezekiel saw some flying saucers a few thousand years ago! Who knows? At least in his vision he saw "a wheel within a wheel" (Ezek. 1:16).

The group divides into one outer circle and one inner circle. Those in the outer circle join hands and move to the right, stepping on the main beats as italicized in the first line of the refrain below. Let them clap their beat before they step to it. Those who form the inner circle are joined together by having each one face left and rest his right hand on the right shoulder of the person ahead of him. Those in the inner circle take light, small steps on the ball of the foot, moving twice as fast as the outer circle. Let them clap the beat. These contrasting speeds of steps are continued through the refrain.

There is also the contrast of the outer circle

• Number 10 in *Look Away: 50 Negro Folk Songs.* Cooperative Recreation Service, Delaware, Ohio. Also in other collections of Negro spirituals.

moving to the right and the inner circle moving to the left. Here is the refrain:

Ezekiel *saw* the *wheel,* 'W*ay up* in the *mid*dle of the *air*,
Ezekiel saw the wheel, 'Way in the middle of the air.
And the big wheel moved by faith, and the little wheel moved by the grace of God,
A wheel in a wheel, 'Way in the middle of the air.

Then this stanza follows:

Some folks like to sing and shout, 'Way in the middle of the air;
Before six months, they'll all turn out, 'Way in the middle of the air.

At the start of this stanza everyone in both circles faces the center standing still, but clapping hands. During the second half of the stanza, those in the outer circle step forward to form the pattern of the former inner circle; those in the inner circle turn out to become the outer circle. While they are changing places, they continue to clap. This time those who had been in the outer circle find that it is a bit more complicated to be in the inner circle. At the start of the refrain again, they should be ready to place the right hand on the right shoulder of the person to the left. So the whole refrain is repeated.

Another stanza is suggested as one for the changing of circles:

Let me tell you what a hypocrite'll do, 'Way in the middle of the air,
He'll talk about me, and he'll talk about you, 'Way in the middle of the air.

All clap as in the previous stanza (not refrain), but as they turn to exchange, they can emphasize "me" and "you." Yes, even fifth- and sixth-graders know the aggravating experience of being talked about—often unfairly. So why not drain off this aggravation with singing and clapping as everyone changes places, perhaps grinning at whomever they pass. Off to the refrain again!

This group pattern may seem to be more fun than educational. True. But children need to feel that they can *enjoy* doing things together and need to *have fun* together. Too often religious emphasis has been presented grimly with the focus on moral perfection covered with a shroud of the past. Surely occasional times can be relished when the group moves gaily, for spontaneous joy is a sign of spiritual and emotional health.

"Go Down, Moses"

This spiritual may be used in its singing form or in Percy Faith's orchestral arrangement. In the orchestral arrangement there seem to be two themes—one involving the enslaved Israelites and one of the Egyptian masters with trumpeters and lashers. The spiritual expresses the strong faith of the Israelites in the midst of despair. It expresses the courage of one man surrounded by a hopeless-yet-hoping group. The children can show a variety of dramatic movements as they experiment in expressing how they would have felt.

Faith Clark of Illinois Teachers College describes how a group of fifth-grade children experimented with "Go Down, Moses":

> They figured out the heavy, oppressed movements of slaves and their fearful reaction to the slave driver. They would rise with the refrain, "Go down, Moses," in pleading movements for their leader to tell the king to set them free. Later, in talking it over, they decided it need not represent just the Hebrew people or Negroes, but the feeling of all oppressed peoples.

HOW WE RELATE TO OTHERS

We need to take time to discover how we relate and interact. Pat Sonen has observed: "To provide for an opportunity for a personality to want to relate his total being to others, requiring him to give and be aware, is an experience of great value in his growing years."

To experiment in relating to others, the group can divide into partners. In each pair, one decides to dramatize the way a person feels (and therefore acts) and the other decides to be the person who shows real understanding, accepting that person, yet having some vision or perspective which may assist the troubled person to feel encouraged. In other words one is to express a distortion; the other person becomes aware, gradually relates, and usually is able to bring more perspective to the troubled one. No speaking, no pulling or pushing—a discipline in awareness growing out of true acceptance.°

This partner interaction should follow some experimenting in the contrast of mood movements on an individual basis.

The one with the problem assumes a dramatic position of distortion and holds it to let the total feeling sink in deeply. The helper should observe and absorb the mood of the other for a while before approaching.

A Lonely Person

Here is an example of action that developed spontaneously between two sixth-grade girls:

Sally decides to act the lonely part so she goes off and stands by herself. Sally's arms are wrapped tightly around her; she looks down. Carol looks at Sally and wonders if she can help Sally not to feel so lonely. . . . Carol comes over to Sally. Carol has understood what it is like when one feels "closed in tight" because of having been hurt. In remembering this Carol finds that she is holding her arms almost as tightly as Sally is holding hers.

° Filmstrip Number 6 in the series "Creative Dramatic Movement," listed on page 74, shows a group of girls improvising in responsive interaction.

But Sally doesn't look up. She even has her feet crossed tightly! Carol parts her arms and lets them rest at her sides. Perhaps Sally notices Carol's hands that are open and perhaps she wonders if Carol really understands.

No, Sally turns away distrustfully. She has been disillusioned about people's being *really* nice. Her foot drags behind her, but her arms are not as tight against her. In fact Carol notices that Sally's hand is free. So she takes a step and very gently slips her hand into Sally's. Sally turns her head a little toward Carol. This time she is not turning away and she may feel that Carol does understand.

All along Carol hasn't known what would evolve; she just wanted to help Sally and all of Carol's actions were sensitive responses to Sally's actions.

Both children were shy, yet sensed a relatedness.

As a leader watching, you can tell when a pair has reached some sort of new relationship and rejoice with them. Life goes on from one adjustment to another and one's awareness of another person may help in just one step of adjusting. After completing this experiment in relatedness, the two reverse parts. The helper acts out some problem and the other one helps.

An Angry Person

Another pair experiments with relating:

Mary stands tense, fists clenched, jaw tight, looking off with a steely gaze. . . . Debbie waits to grasp some understanding of Mary's mood before approaching her. Then she comes up to Mary, a little in front of her. Debbie sees Mary's anger and bitterness. Debbie recalls times when she has been angry and frustrated and as she thinks of those times she finds that her fists are clenched too. . . . But Mary looks right past Debbie with a hard, steady gaze. . . . Debbie feels more tense and raises her clenched fists at the line of Mary's vision.

She tries to communicate her feeling that there is a lot that is wrong in this world and that we all get furious. . . . Mary steps back as she sees Debbie so intense with this feeling of frustration. But Mary is still hostile. . . . Debbie can't seem to get out of her mood of frustration. She is at a loss to think of some other expressive action, but she looks straight at Mary. . . . Mary feels her tenseness drain off, either because of Debbie's tenseness or just because of the natural reaction of fatigue from muscle tension. . . . Her hand goes up to her head in a bewildered gesture. She is beginning to see Debbie as someone who is acquainted with the hostile world too. . . . Instead of being all wrapped up in hostility, Mary is becoming aware of her own self.

All of a sudden Debbie gives a thrust forward and opens her hands as if to express the idea that we have to let these frustrations drain off. After all we can't go around with continuous bitterness. Mary is a bit skeptical, but her hand, which was clenched, is now open! Debbie reaches out to Mary's open hand and Mary finds that her hand is reaching out to Debbie's. . . .

• • •

This sequence is described, not to be followed, but to show how two persons related to each other. They were improvising and they would never do it exactly that way again, but they were learning to be more aware of other people.

One Who Feels Apart from the Group

The children discuss how alone they have felt when they have gone to a camp or changed schools, and so on. They remember someone who helped them so that they hadn't felt so lonely. What can one do when there is a new girl at school? (We found that ten- and eleven-year-old girls were more interested in these problems than the boys of this age; so we did

FIGURE 17

not urge the boys to join us at this time.) Are there very shy girls at school? Can we help them to feel at ease?

The group reads some lines that are written on the chalkboard: "She sits alone. . . . Why won't she join us? . . . Perhaps—if one of us goes instead of a bunch. . . . Look! They're coming back! Make room for her in our circle!" What could be happening "between the lines"?

The group decides that it will experiment with dramatic movement. (If the group is over twelve in number, there could be a division into smaller groups of six to nine each, having the lines on a piece of paper. Then after a given time of experimenting each group could bring back its unique interpretation to share with the others.)

This is what one group worked out:

Carol sits alone at one side. On the other side is a group of eight girls in a circle . . . their heads together. One may be saying, "Why

won't she join us?" . . . Two decide to go to Carol to tell her that she can come over to their group—if she wants to.

They stand over Carol, but Carol doesn't feel they really want her. One stands with her hands on her hips; the other leans over with her fingers extended sharp as spikes. Carol turns her back on them; she wishes she could get away (Figure 17). . . . The girls leave Carol and return to their group.

Nancy has been watching. She knows how it feels to be alone, so she goes to Carol and sits down beside her. Nancy looks down, pretending that she has found something unusual. Carol looks at it. Their hands meet as Nancy offers it to Carol. . . . Nancy wants to get Carol up from the floor, so she imagines something of interest that is away from the group. . . . Carol gets up to see what Nancy is interested in. . . . Nancy suddenly decides to bring Carol to the group. She takes Nancy's hand and the spontaneous action seems to be accepted by Carol. As they approach, the group makes room for them.

● ● ●

The children are learning a lot about sensitive thoughtfulness of others. They may plan other "problems," such as making up after a quarrel. The leader gets to know the children more deeply in this type of creative communication—learns their fears, frustrations, desires, needs. And the children get to know themselves and others in a deeper dimension.

The children are learning the Golden Rule in a new way. The Golden Rule might be paraphrased and expanded as: Use your imagination. Imagine how you would want to be treated; see how it would feel by acting it out with another. So in a real situation, be ready to use your imagination and do what you would want another to do to you.

There may be an involvement of a variety of groups. Pat Sonen offers an example:

Sometimes it takes lots of talk and planning by the class to "boil down the idea" that will be used. A teacher of a class of twelve-year-olds said she found herself acting as moderator with her class as they planned a movement story on the theme of the "Big City."

One boy felt they should divide into small groups first. The teacher asked if they should be separate boys' and girls' groups, or mixed groups. Quickly a girl replied, "Mixed of course. All the people in cities are mixed in their groups." Then the teacher followed this idea: "What kind of groups will we have in our Big City?" After much planning the class decided to have five groups:

A group of poor people—the laborers
A group of the wealthy—who ran the city
A group of thieves—who were destructive
A group of old and sick—who needed to be cared for
A group of visitors—thinking of moving into the city

A general plan was made, the groups were formed, and they retired to different parts of the room to work out their portion of the dance story. The general plan had a beginning, a middle part, and an end.

Twenty minutes later the entire class came into the center of the room, with some rushing about, moving in various directions to give the feeling of the hustle of city life. They brought this exciting movement to an end as they found their appointed groups.

Then the group of visitors began an inspection tour of the city. As they went from group to group they observed the action of each, and its effect on the others. In the end the visitors came away to make the decision. . . . They decided to come there to live, so returned to the groups and were welcomed in movement as they did so. Then as in the beginning the city as a whole became alive again with the motion of its daily life.

Perhaps this story could be expanded to have the group of visitors be a concerned group. After the welcome in movement, could there be some awareness between the separate groups as a result of the new group (formerly visitors) who sense a related whole in life? Experiment also with a change of pace for a time of worship on a Sunday or on any day. Time for God is needed even in the hustle of city life. How can this be shown?

2

CREATING GROUP DESIGNS WITH SYMBOLIC MOVEMENT

INTERPRETING HYMNS

"In Christ There Is No East or West"

Children of this age study other countries, and they enjoy representing people from all over the world. Using the poem of John Oxenham, which is in most hymnals, one group of children decided to use the first stanza as a grand chain of greeting°:

In Christ there is no East or West,
In him no South or North;
But one great fellowship of love
Throughout the whole wide earth.

Although this group of children decided to use a circle design, there are many other ways of interpreting this hymn, for each group will have ideas to express the special meaning for that particular group at that particular time.

It is ideal if there can be children of various races and nationalities, but if this is not possible, children can wear some suggestion of a costume such as a scarf, a shawl, a hat, or a flower lei.

If the children decide on a circle design with a "grand chain" of greeting, they stand in a circle and number off: "one, two, one, two."

Each "one" turns to the right and extends his right hand to his adjacent "two" who has

° Described in Filmstrip Number 7, listed on page 74.

turned to his left. Then the group is ready to make a grand chain of greeting as the first stanza is sung. If there are about twelve in the circle, they will go all the way around the circle and return to the place where they started.

STANZA TWO:

Join hands, then, brothers of the faith,
Whate'er your race may be.
Who serves my Father as a son
Is surely kin to me.

For the first half, everyone joins hands and circles to the left.

Who serves my Father: With hands no longer joined, all reach up, center—hands high and parallel.

As a son: Lower arms and widen them to the sides.

Is surely kin to me: Clasp hand of the second person on either side—not the hands of the adjacent persons (Figure 18).

STANZA THREE:

In him shall true hearts everywhere: "Twos" take step forward toward center, hands in prayer position. "Ones" take step backward and kneel, hands in prayer position.

Their high communion find: "Twos" take step forward and have weight forward as they lift their praying hands slowly and steadily toward a high center. They look above their

FIGURE 18

praying hands. It is as if they are building a prayer chapel. "Ones" stay kneeling, watching this "prayer chapel."

His service is the golden cord: "Twos" lower hands and take a step backward. "Ones" rise and take a step forward.

Close-binding all mankind: Friendship ring is formed by everyone in one circle standing closely together with arms crossed in front and hands grasping the hands of adjacent persons.

This pattern for "In Christ There Is No East or West" was used at a mass meeting at the fairgrounds in Sacramento, California to welcome Frank Laubach. The participants—thirty-four people of twenty different racial and national backgrounds including Mexicans, Negroes, Japanese, and Chinese—moved in this pattern of world friendship. Before it was presented, these remarks were made: "We hope our audience will, in spirit, join this world-inclusive circle, and not only feel and sing these sentiments, but also put all of them into glori-

ous action wherever they go." Group symbolic designs offer a chance for those observing to identify with the interpreters.

Sixth- and seventh-graders have presented this as a part of the observance of the World Day of Prayer.

The fourth stanza may be interpreted with a repetition of the grand chain, ending in one wide circle with hands joined.

Help the children to realize that there are Christians all around the world—yes, in Russia too. Also remind them to smile as they reach out to others, for a smile communicates friendliness anywhere in the world.

"For the Beauty of the Earth"

Creative dramatic movement may be described as "finger painting" in space. In using "For the Beauty of the Earth" the children should be encouraged to consider what the main idea is in a line or two or in a whole stanza. "For the beauty of the earth" might be some movement in the lower area contrasted

55

by a related movement in the higher area for "for the glory of the skies." After free experimenting, they might like to try their movements standing in a group design of an inverted V formation, all facing toward a worship center. If they divide into groups of eight, there would be four on each side—the top pair would be closer to the worship center and closer together; the fourth pair would be farthest apart and be farthest from the worship center. The words of the hymn might be on the chalkboard or on large sheets of paper on an easel.

STANZA ONE:

For the beauty of the earth,°
For the glory of the skies,
For the love which from our birth,
Over and around us lies,

REFRAIN: Lord of all, to thee we raise
This our hymn of grateful praise.

For the beauty of the earth: Action of beauty (low movement).†
For the glory of the skies: Action of wonder of sky—clouds, stars (high movement).
For the love which from our birth over and around us lies: Some low surrounding or enclosing gesture growing into high, extended and surrounding gesture.
Lord of all: Some humble posture, allowing for a rising gesture during "to thee we raise." If the group is in inverted V formation, the fourth couple may come forward up the middle to the worship center with arms uplifted during "this our hymn of grateful praise." The others just hold their hands upraised and face the worship center. The fourth pair remains top center.

° This hymn was written by Folliott Sanford Pierpoint, 1835-1917.
† Various interpretations for this stanza are discussed on pp. 82-85.

STANZA TWO:

For the wonder of each hour of the day and of the night: The group can spread out and also make all-inclusive gestures of time.
Hill and vale, and tree and flower, sun and moon, and stars of light: In such a fast succession of word pictures, it is better to build this with individual movement—one or two for various parts: "hill and vale" (space), "tree and flower" (growing things), "sun and moon and stars" (constellations). These three sections may develop in sequence with special symbolic movements, so the group is all involved with three distinct variations. Then all join in the repetition of the refrain of praise. This time the third couple that is then farthest from the worship center now moves forward as the fourth pair did on the first refrain.

STANZA THREE:

For the joy of human love, brother, sister, parent, child: Two circles are formed—one on the right and one on the left—hands joined and held high. Those in both circles move until they have returned to the place where they started.
Friends on earth: Those on the right look across and those on the left look across toward opposite partner; both sides reach toward each other with "upstage" arms.
And friends above: Everyone looks up and lifts outstretched horizontal arm to vertical position or high diagonal line.
For all gentle thoughts and mild: Each one brings the upraised arm down on a curve that leads him into a turning "downstage," around to the outside and up toward the worship center. Then all are ready to repeat the refrain, with the second couple coming up center with upraised arms.

STANZA FOUR:

For thy church that evermore lifteth holy hands above: The two tallest children or two

56

FIGURE 19

boys, should be the couple that has just come up center on the previous refrain. These two face the worship center, lift their inside hands on high diagonal so that fingertips touch as if forming the peaked roof of a church. The outside arms are in a downward angle, slightly out from the body. The palm is down. The other six kneel and lift "praying hands" during the singing of this line.

Offering up on every shore: Following the worship symbolism, there now may be the symbolism of benevolent, outgoing work of the church. So the center top two face each other, bring their outside hands up to the peak made by their touching inside hands. As they do this the center two lower the former inside hands and turn away from the worship center with outward gesture by extending the free arm. At the same time the six who had been kneeling rise. They lower the praying hands, turn and face outward, and reach outward with concern for people everywhere.

Her pure sacrifice of love: The upper two hold their position; the other six take two steps outward and reach with more extension (Figure 19). Then for the closing refrain the couple farthest out (should be the original first pair) moves toward the worship center, as all turn with uplifted arms. During the "Amen" the hands may come together in the prayer position.

This design offers varied actions for the stanzas, but always returns to the same design for the refrain except that each time the succes-

FIGURE 20   FIGURE 21

sive couple approaches the worship center.

Take time to discuss the singing of the refrain with a feeling of thankfulness. Usually one says "Thank you" with a smile, so this refrain should be sung with a feeling of joy.

• • •

This hymn is interpreted for Thanksgiving time, for World Day of Prayer services and for any service of worship. See what original ideas your group will bring to the interpretation of this hymn.

• • •

Lucy Haywood, a teacher in weekday religious education, writes:

A group of girls got together at noon recess to act out some of "For the Beauty of the Earth." Later in class the boys said, "Why didn't we get to do it?" So I said, "Four of you go out in the hall with the copy of this stanza and see what you can work out." I knew it was a gamble for they were four mischiefs, but they came back and gave a reverent and meaningful interpretation as we sang the stanza. We use dramatic movement only a little, but it is a powerful thing.

"All Creatures of Our God and King"

Francis of Assisi and his followers sang and used gestures to express their joy in all of God's creation. "All Creatures of Our God and King," which is attributed to Saint Francis, is an early antiphonal hymn. It can be interpreted antiphonally by two groups, possibly at opposite sides of a room. Group A takes the lead phrase and Group B echoes the movement of Group A—except for variations in the first two lines and the unison action of the final line.

A—*All creatures of our God and King:* Low movement (Figure 20).

B—*Lift up your voice and with us sing:* High movement.

A—*Alleluia:* Sweeping movement (Figure 21).

B—*Alleluia:* Sweeping movement.

A—*Thou burning sun with golden beam:* Wide circle.

B—*Thou silver moon with softer gleam:* Similar but more protracted.

58

A—*O praise him:* Gesture of praise.
B—*O praise him:* Gesture of praise.
A—*Alleluia:* Swing or turn.
B—*Alleluia:* Swing or turn.
A and B—*Alleluia:* Swing or turn into one group.

Group B should have a chance to set the movement patterns and let Group A echo their movements.

The stanza that begins "Thou rushing wind that art so strong, ye clouds that sail in heaven along" can be interpreted similarly except for the first two lines. Both groups move at once. Those in Group A hold their arms high and rounded as cumulus clouds, slowly turning. Those in Group B are the "rushing wind." They run lightly with weight forward as they weave in and out among the "clouds." All return to original places by the end of the couplet. The design for the first stanza is used for the rest of this stanza.

Fifth- and sixth-graders have interpreted another stanza in this way:

A—*All you who are of tender heart:* Turn to partner with "Peace" gesture of the Church of South India. (Two place their right hands palm to palm, then place the left hand over the partner's right. This is the symbolic gesture of Christian fellowship. See page 69.)

B—*Forgiving others, take your part:* Same "Peace" gesture.

A—*Alleluia:* Swing toward center.

B—*Alleluia:* Swing toward center.

A—*You who do pain and sorrow bear:* Kneel as if crushed by discouragement.

B—*Praise God and on him cast your care:* Although the start is with an upward look, follow with kneeling, with hands low but outstretched to suggest the giving over of burdens.

The previous design is used for the rest of the stanza.

Group A could be an all-boy group and choose their own interpretations. Group B could be an all-girl group and choose their own interpretations—not feeling obliged to echo Group A.

•   •   •

In the filmstrip "All Creatures of our God and King"* a group of fifth- and sixth-graders interpret this hymn in a single circle. Sometimes it is done in concentric circles. It can be interpreted in many ways.

The greatest value in this hymn is the opportunity to move to joyous "alleluias." Help the children to lift through the diaphragm, the head, the eyes—to express joyous praise through their whole being.

"Praise and Thanksgiving"

The children learned the devotional round "Praise and Thanksgiving"† and were able to sing it as a round. They decided to experiment with its interpretation in a small chapel.

Praise and thanksgiving let everyone bring: Two on each side came down the outside aisles. Their hands were uplifted in the gesture of bringing praise and thanksgiving for all the blessings of God.

Unto our Father for every good thing: They approached the altar and knelt but decided to look up in thanks. (It seemed to them that the bowed head looked more penitent than thankful.)

All together joyfully sing: They rose and turned in close to each other. Then as they started out the center aisle, they heeded the lilt that is in the music and took running steps with arms uplifted during "joyfully sing." Their discussion included the idea that after kneeling they could go out with a new energy and joy.

---

* Filmstrip Number 8, listed on page 74.
† Described in Filmstrip Number 8, listed on page 74.

PRAISE AND THANKSGIVING

Paraphrase of the German

Lobet und Preiset
Alsatian Round

I. Praise and thanks-gi-ving let eve-ry-one bring Un-to our

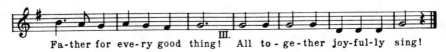

Fa-ther for eve-ry good thing! All to-ge-ther joy-ful-ly sing!

"Praise and Thanksgiving" from *The Whole World Singing* by Edith Lovell Thomas. Copyrighted 1950 by Friendship Press, New York, N. Y. Used by permission.

Since this is a three-part round, Group 1 started down the side aisles on the first line. Group 1 knelt on the second line, while Group 2 came down the side aisles. Group 1 rose and came out the center aisle on the third line; Group 2 knelt on the second line; and Group 3 started down the side aisles. Group 1 started to repeat the round and its action—and so it went through two complete cycles. Children love to interpret rounds. Since this would involve six at a time, the others might sing the three-part round while sitting in the chapel. The round could involve twelve children if pairs entered on both sides instead of single persons, and if the center aisle has space for four to leave together.

•   •   •

There are many hymns that can be interpreted with dramatic action. Those with refrains or moods are preferable to many that are involved in intellectual theories.

Imagine the action as you sing the words of hymns[*]:

All hail the power of Jesus' name,
  Let angels prostrate fall!

---
[*] "All Hail the Power of Jesus' Name," "Once to Every Man and Nation," and "Were You There?"

By the light of burning martyrs,
  Jesus' bleeding feet I track,
Toiling up new Calvaries ever.

Sometimes it causes me to tremble, tremble, tremble,
Were you there when they crucified my Lord?

Imagine action to portray the moods of some hymn tunes:

Picardy—"Let All Mortal Flesh Keep Silence"

Ebenezer (Ton-Y-Botel)—"Once to Every Man and Nation"

Ein' Feste Burg—"A Mighty Fortress Is Our God"

Grand Isle—"I Sing a Song of the Saints of God"

Hymn to Joy—"Joyful, Joyful, We Adore Thee"

Cwm Rhondda—"God of Grace and God of Glory"

From now on hymns will have a new dimension! Not all hymns are right for action. But there will be so many that take on new meaning because with your imagination you will be *living the hymn* even though you are standing with hymnbook in hand, appearing quite conventional!

60

INTERPRETING CHRISTMAS CAROLS

"O Holy Night"

The French carol "O Holy Night" can serve for a processional of "angels," or worshipers. The first stanza sets the feeling of expectancy as the group approaches a worship center.

In the refrain, "Fall on your knees" suggests kneeling. Then while kneeling the worshipers can have an upward and open expression of listening during "O hear the angel voices." During "O night divine . . ." the group rises and on the special high emphases, the group may be circling with right hands touching and reaching upward. The mood is that of mystery.

"While by My Sheep" or "The Echo Song"

Children enjoy an echo song or a repetition of a design. The early German carol "While by My Sheep" can be interpreted in various ways: in the design of two concentric circles, in two groups, or in two levels or two areas. Since so much of it is antiphonal, it can have an echo in the movement and the sustaining of some gesture while the alternate group moves.

With the repetition of "joy," the children will do a lot of experimenting in movements of joy. The "joy" in this carol is close in meaning to "surprising joy" or "something wonderful." Let the children feel this through their mind, soul, and body—through the eyes and mouth and the lift of diaphragm and the head —with a quick inbreathing, before singing the words. So hearts are lifted to the Lord.

Since this is a shepherd's song, it could be done with boys only. Or the boys could take the first line; the girls, the second; and so on.

"Go Tell It on the Mountain"

"Go Tell It on the Mountain"° is a jubilant Christmas spiritual with a dynamic start for the group in the opening line of the refrain. After the refrain, during the stanza, one or two may carry the mood while the others remain still, perhaps kneeling. This carol appeals to boys with its energetic emphasis and with a stanza about a watchman, and no angels. It could be done by boys only.

There is a place for a leap and running during "Go tell it on the mountain, over the hills and everywhere! Go tell it on the mountain." Then comes the amazing "good news": "that Jesus Christ is born!" The music seems to stress "Jesus Christ" so the last part of the phrase could express quiet wonder. The general pattern should be worked out according to the space and the decision of the group.

"The Holly and the Ivy"

"The Holly and the Ivy,"° a traditional English carol, was originally interpreted as a folk dance on the village green during the twelve days of Christmas festivities. It may have been done in a circle form or as a contra dance, but since no notations have come down we are free to create any variations on English folk dance patterns or to use any pattern of our own.

If wreaths are used, the boys or those in the inside circle are the ones who hold the wreaths. The inside circle is called the "holly" and may wear a sprig of holly. The outer circle is called the "ivy."

The holly and the ivy: The "holly" ones face out to their partners. "Ivy" ones touch the wreaths held out by the "holly" ones. They balance forward and back toward each other. Right arms raised; weight goes forward on right feet, then back onto left feet.

When they are: Each couple balances forward.

° In *Little Book of Carols*, p. 24. Cooperative Recreation Service, Delaware, Ohio.

° In *Little Book of Carols*, p. 9. Cooperative Recreation Service. This carol is described in Filmstrip Number 6, listed on page 74.

WHILE BY MY SHEEP

Allegretto

From the German

1. While by my sheep I watched at night, Glad tid-ings brought an an - gel bright.
2. There shall be born, so he did say, In Beth - le - hem a Child to - day;
3. There shall the Child lie in a stall, This Child who shall re-deem us all.
4. This gift of God I'll cher - ish well, That ev - er joy my heart shall fill.

How great my joy! Great my joy! Joy, joy, joy! Joy, joy, joy!

Praise we the Lord in Heav'n on high! Praise we the Lord in Heav'n on high!

Both full grown: With right hands on wreath held high, couples progress halfway around until they are in the opposite position. The "ivy" ones now are facing out and the "holly" ones are on the outside.

Of all the trees: The "ivy" ones lift both arms forward and upward so that the rounded arms are directly overhead. In all the other stanzas the words for this line will be: "And Mary bore." (So, for a moment, each girl expresses the wonder of Mary.) The "holly" kneels on one knee, back straight, wreath resting on the knee. The attention is on the girls' arms.

That are in the wood: The girls widen their arms and lower them to their sides. The girls, or "ivy" continue to look up throughout this line. In all the following stanzas, the words for this line are: "Sweet Jesus Christ." The quiet, slow movement adds to the spiritual emphasis.

The holly: "Holly" rises and reaches forward with wreath. "Ivy" touches wreath as it is elevated.

Bears the crown: With the wreath high, each couple moves in a close circle right until the two are back in their original positions.

REFRAIN:

The rising of: "Holly" makes a quarter turn to the left; the "ivy" makes a quarter turn to her right and touches the wreath with her left hand. So all the couples are facing clockwise in a double circle. Wreaths are held shoulder high or a little higher. The turning into this circle takes the first part of this phrase and then two light steps follow.

The sun: "Holly" progresses two steps. "Ivy" breaks contact with the wreath, turns away from the partner, out and around and back to the inner circle, but during this time the "holly" has taken two steps, so the "ivy" finds a new partner—the one right behind her previous partner. She touches his wreath.

And the running of: The couples progress.

The deer: "Holly" progresses two steps, while "ivy" turns out to the right and back as during "the sun." A new partner is found again and she touches his wreath.

The playing of: Couples progress.

The merry organ: Same pattern of girls' turning out to the right and returning to a new partner.

Sweet singing in the choir: Partners progress, but stand still as they sing "choir."

Then everyone turns to face his partner, and repeats the entire design for successive stanzas and the refrain.

INTERPRETING EASTER CAROLS

"Love Is Come Again"

"Love Is Come Again"° is an early sixteenth-century carol based on a traditional French carol "Noël nouvelet." Its use of the word love is to symbolize Christ; in more recent times we have used this term in some of our hymns: "Love's redeeming work is done," "Love divine, all loves excelling," and "O Love that wilt not let me go."

• • •

Now the green blade riseth from the buried
 grain,
Wheat that in dark earth many days has
 lain;
Love lives again, that with the dead has
 been:

REFRAIN: Love is come again,
   Like wheat that springeth green.

Forth he came at Easter, like the risen
 grain,
He that for three days in the grave had lain,
Quick from the dead my risen Lord is seen:

° Number 149 in *The Oxford Book of Carols.* Also the Fusner arrangement in *Church Music Review,* Number 2232. H. W. Gray Co., New York, N. Y. *Also in the Methodist Hymnal as #441 Now The Green Blade Riseth.*

FIGURE 22

When our hearts are wintry, grieving or in
pain,
Thy touch can call us back to life again,
Fields of our hearts that dead and bare have
been:

REFRAIN

Because of the elementary mystery of a grain
of wheat being buried and then miraculously
thrusting up its green blade, this carol which
uses such imagery is valuable with children.
The comparison acts as a bridge between the
mystery of things that are seen and the mystery
of things that are not seen.

In the second stanza the third line is stabbed
with quick awareness of the risen Christ—at
that moment on Easter morning and forever.

In the last stanza the children gather that
there is a Power which is available to them,
constantly, in any dark times. This carol
touches upon the promise that wintry seasons
will be followed by growing seasons, that the
Eternal undergirds mankind with amazing renewal of energy. So man continually rejoices
in the refrain: "Love is come again, like wheat
that springeth green."

The extremely simple and stylized pattern
suggested for this carol allows it to be a medi-
tative pathway because the mind does not
have any complex movements to follow. Also
the same pattern is repeated for all three
stanzas except for the third line of the second
stanza.

The basic step of three steps forward and
one step backward is the *tripudium* referred
to many times in early Christian processions.
In 1682 Father Menestrier wrote that "on
Easter Day, in a number of churches he himself had seen canons and choristers holding
hands and dancing to the singing of joyous
hymns." There is a value in reliving some of
the designs of choral movement in the early
church, just as there is value in seeing the art
and singing the chants of the historical Christian church.

• • •

Everyone is in one circle or in concentric
circles if the group is large. Everyone kneels
with the left knee on the floor, the right knee
up. The hands are at the sides, slightly outward.

Now the green blade riseth: Each one slowly
brings his hands together as "praying hands"

or a "green blade"; then lifts the hands vertically so that they are at forehead height.

From the buried grain: Hands part, push out to the sides so that palms touch the palms of the adjacent persons. The hands are now at the side at ear level (Figure 22).

Wheat that in dark earth: With hands remaining in the contact position, everyone rises onto the right foot on "wheat"; then takes two more steps to the right—left on "that" and right foot on "dark." Then the weight is shifted back to the left foot on "earth."

Many days has lain: The same design continues with right, left, right and left back.

Love lives again: As if each one is a spoke from the hub of a wheel, each one makes a quarter turn to the right so that he may progress on this radius outward away from the center. The right foot turns out on "love"; left on "lives"; right on "gain"; then rest back on the left. As each one turns, he draws the hands together at chest level.

That with the dead has been: This phrase is used for making a turn in place. Right foot forward; then pivot to the right. As this turn is made the hands separate and spread downward and out at the side. Each one looks down. Weight goes back on left foot. Everyone is now facing the center.

REFRAIN:

Love is come again: Each one takes a breath —feeling a lift in the diaphragm—head up; then takes three steps forward into the center, starting with the right foot. The hands are in praying position at chin level. Everyone looks up with expectancy.

Like wheat that springeth green: "Like"— Balancing back onto the left foot, everyone lowers the hands a little. "Wheat that"—Each one lifts diaphragm; hands separate and push out horizontally to the sides at shoulder level as in the second half of the first line ("from the buried grain"). "Springeth"—All adjacent palms touch. "Green"—All hands in contact are lifted slightly above head level. The head is back and the focus of the eyes is high center to express an awareness of mystery.

The second stanza is the same except for the design in the third line:

Quick from the dead: Everyone turns out from the center with the same three steps forward and one back as described for line three in the first stanza. But the variation is that this time the praying hands are held at forehead level.

My risen Lord is seen: The same turn is made to the right as in line three of the first stanza but, just as the turn is completed, the hands which have been held high now separate as if in a burst of surprise.

•   •   •

This carol has been interpreted in chancels at early morning family services of worship. The children wear the same choir gowns as the children's singing choir. The choir sings the carol for the interpreting choir.

This same pattern may be used for the Christmas words written for this carol originally:

Sing Noel, ye people,
    sing your joyful praise,
Fill the air with gladness;
    let your voices raise,
Carols of joy to Christ,
    our newborn King.
Sing Noel, ye people,
    rejoice through all your days.

Join the choir of angels,
    now over Bethlehem,
Chanting, "Peace on earth
    and happiness to men."
Come see the Babe,
    behold your newborn King.
Sing Noel, ye people,
    sing Noel again.

65

In a humble manger
   he lies and close beside
Gracious Mary watches,
   smiles with gentle pride,
Smiles at her Babe, at Christ,
   our newborn King.
Sing Noel, ye people,
   may Christ with you abide.

"An Easter Carol"

Here is a joyous Easter anthem—"An Easter Carol"°—sung by children's choirs offering both variety and simplicity, using an entire group or just a few children. At times everyone sings; at other times a soloist or a few voices; and at other times antiphonal groups sing.

•   •   •

Choir:
      Alleluia, Alleluia,
Shout the news to all the earth,
Christ is risen, Christ is risen,
   giving life a second birth.

The interpreting choir expresses the excitement of the news of the risen Christ.

Solo:

Tell it in Gethsemane, where Jesus knelt to pray,
Tell it in Joseph's garden, where Jesus' body lay,
Tell it to a mourning world, weeping o'er its dead,
Tell them Jesus rose today, and all our fears have fled.

For each line a different one (or two) may interpret the mood, moving expressively; then merging back into the group.

° In *Church Music Review,* Number 1966. H. W. Gray Co., New York, N. Y.

Choir:
  Alleluia, Alleluia, Christ is risen, Christ is risen,
  Christ is risen, Christ is risen, Alleluia, Alleluia,
      Christ is risen today!

Here the group may move antiphonally as the music suggests with the alternating of soprano and alto parts.

Solo:

Bring the news to every nation,
Bring them living words of cheer,
Tell them Jesus died to save us,
Tell them death has lost its fear.

Two or four may move out from the group as if to invite others into their rejoicing group. Interlude: Four bars without words; music has an ascending quality.

Those who had reached out may actually bring in some others or may imagine that they are bringing others and go toward a worship center.

Choir:
  Alleluia, Alleluia, Christ is risen, Christ is risen,
  Christ is risen, Christ is risen, Alleluia, Alleluia,
  Alleluia, Alleluia, Christ is risen today!

•   •   •

The joyous climax may be antiphonal design with wide swings, spiral turns, and so on. Then on "today" the group comes to a climax of the "now" mood, communicating the message as affecting us *in this moment* and not as a song of a past historical event. An exultant thrust that is sustained—powerful, total.

"Christ the Lord Is Risen Today"

"Christ the Lord Is Risen Today," the well-known Easter hymn with its "alleluias" at the close of each line, can be interpreted simply and joyously.° Boys should be encouraged to interpret this hymn with strong announcing movements. On that first Easter morning the angels were "men in shining raiment."

• • •

Christ the Lord is risen today: Announcing gesture.

Alleluia: A wide, rejoicing gesture.

Sons of men and angels say: Contrasting of low to high movement.

Alleluia: Turning; arms high except toward the end of the phrase when they are lowered, but the diaphragm and head are up.

Raise your joys and triumphs high: Walk in some forward pattern with arms starting to lift gradually but reaching a high thrust on "high."

Alleluia: Joyous, free turning.

Sing, ye heavens, and earth reply: Contrasting movements from high to low.

Alleluia: The fullest spiral turning into a high thrust, with a sense of rejoicing shining through the face as it is felt through the whole being.

• • •

These "alleluias" need to be expressed totally by children so that as they sing them in the more reserved surrounding of a conventional worship service, they may be moving imaginatively and feel deeply involved with the mood, although there is no visible expression unless it be the lift of the diaphragm and the head. The early Christians were known as a joyous people, mainly because of the experience of Easter. They had no hymnals or prayer books, but they used gestures. The children should be encouraged to be totally involved in expressing this exultation as a part of their heritage from the early church. The meaning communicated into the depth of their being is that the wonder of Easter can never be expressed in words

---

° An explanation of the use of this hymn for adults is given in *Look Up and Live,* pp. 82-88.

alone, but in joyous response to the living Christ today.

INTERPRETING THE LORD'S PRAYER

The children are old enough to think deeply into the meaning of the Lord's Prayer. Carol Warner tells of her first venture in dramatic and symbolic movement with upper grade school children who interpreted this prayer for a Children's Day Service of Worship:

> Four girls were selected and work began on the Lord's Prayer. . . . We had carefully talked about the meaning of each phrase and had realized that by interpreting this prayer in movements they were praying not only for themselves but for the congregation as well. . . . It was a deeply moving religious experience for each of them and for every member of the congregation.

Worship "must not be considered solely as a verbal expression of a religious impulse, but as a total behavior pattern in which posture and active gesture are as much a part of the whole as the verbal or mental imagery." Paul wrote to Timothy: "I desire . . . that in every place . . . men should pray, lifting holy hands" (1 Tim. 2:8).

There are innumerable ways of interpreting the Lord's Prayer. Members of a group will always have some new ideas to share, so that each group feels: "This is *our* interpretation." And one might add, "Yes, at this time," for the same group will keep changing certain movements as understanding grows. The following are suggestions. Feel free to use any of the ideas or none of them.

• • •

This design is in the form of a circle of prayer. If the group is large, it can be done with concentric circles that have a common center of devotion, a center that is above them, that lifts their vision.

The interpretation may be done to a variety of backgrounds: music; slowly spoken words; antiphonal readings with an explanatory phrase after each portion or each phrase; phrases said by the leader, and then repeated by the group as they interpret it; and so on.

Our Father: Everyone is kneeling with hands in prayer gesture. TIME OF CENTERING.

Who art in heaven: The praying hands lift and separate. There is an openness. TIME OF AWARENESS.

Hallowed be thy name: The arms are now drawn in and down; head is bowed—aware of God's power beyond man's understanding. TIME OF HUMILITY.

Thy kingdom come: Each one straightens his back and raises his head. He gets onto the right knee and then to a standing position. On "come" there is a full extension of the right hand. TIME OF VISION.

Thy will be done: The vision is still high as the left arm is lifted parallel to the right. TIME OF PETITION.

On earth: Hands are lowered and everyone looks down. The palms are down with a gesture of concern for the world and the place where one stands. (Surely Jesus urged his disciples to pray for God's will to be done on earth because he believed it was possible.) TIME OF COMMITMENT.

As it is in heaven: Everyone looks up. The arms are in an open position at the sides; shoulders down, head back but resting without strain. (The group is open to consider the perfection of God's will.) TIME OF CONTEMPLATION.

Give us this day: Each one takes one step toward the center with an upward gesture of petition with palms up ready to receive. TIME OF CONCERN FOR DAILY NEEDS.

Our daily bread: The arms widen sideward so that each person's wrist touches the wrist of his neighbor's. Here is an interlinking of prayerful concern for everyone around the world. Each one should look to his right to see that his right wrist touches the wrist of his neighbor's at the right. In this way the design unfolds without anyone's having to look to the left. TIME OF WORLD CONCERN.

And forgive us our debts: Each one draws his hands, in clenched position, toward his chest and lets them rest against his chest (traditional gesture for admitting one's own faults). The head is bowed and the knees are bent slightly. TIME OF CONTRITION.

As we forgive our debtors: Each one reaches with his right arm almost touching the back of the person to his right. He steps to the right as he reaches to the right. Toward the end of the phrase, he reaches a little farther with a feeling of loving forgiveness. And while he is absorbed in this reach beyond himself, he is being forgiven at the same time by the person at his left. So the law of forgiveness is symbolized first in the need for penitent seeking of God's forgiveness, then balanced by the outreaching forgiveness toward others. TIME OF FORGIVENESS.

And lead us: Each one steps into the center with the left foot; hands are clasped with fingers folded over to express prayer of agony and need, and they are lifted toward the center to symbolize that they need a power above their own. TIME OF NEED.

Not into temptation: Realizing that temptation is the pull away from God's will, each one admits his awareness of this pull by turning away from the center, hands still clasped, right elbow leading in a downward twist. TIME OF ADMISSION TO TEMPTATION.

But deliver us: Immediately the group remembers that deliverance is always possible with God. Everyone turns back to the center, clasped hands lifted even higher; the head is back. TIME OF COMPLETE TURNING TO GOD.

From evil: Each one steps back onto his right foot. He brings hands down on "from" to chest level, then lets hands separate and continue down to sides of body; palms face out. Temptation is over and behind. As the hands reach full downward extension, the chest is lifted and the head is raised in serenity. TIME OF FAITH IN GOD'S SALVATION.

For thine is the kingdom: During "thine" everyone brings hands together in the prayer gesture at head level. The weight is forward on the left foot; head is high. During "kingdom" the arms widen with a high thrust—full diagonal extension, slightly backward to suggest openness. TIME OF AFFIRMATION.

And the power: Each one makes a half turn to the right so that he faces outward. As he turns, he draws his hands down close to the chest, but on "power" he thrusts them out strongly on a forward diagonal extension. TIME OF SENSING GOD'S POWER EVERYWHERE.

And the glory: The arms are lifted from the high diagonal thrust to a curved high circle directly overhead. Then each one completes the turn around to the right until everyone is facing toward the center. The group looks up with a sense of glory. TIME OF WONDER.

Forever: The arms widen out to the sides—horizontal at shoulder level—to symbolize the endless circle of eternity. TIME OF SENSING THE ETERNAL.

Amen: Everyone brings his hands together in prayer with an upward look and kneels. ("Amen" means "may this be so" and after such a powerful prayer, it is better for the group not to bow the head, because it suggests an ending or closing down, whereas those who have been praying should feel full of energy to join with God's power to see that this prayer "may be so." The group kneels, but is ready to rise and go out with new clarity and power.) TIME OF COMMITMENT.

•   •   •

Here is an example of antiphonal-explanatory readings:

Give us this day: We ask for the gift of daily care.

Our daily bread: And we would share our daily bread with others.

And forgive us our debts: Forgive us our failures and our selfish acts.

As we forgive our debtors: As we forgive others with understanding love.

The children should make up their own explanatory remarks, of course.

•   •   •

In some places in our country dramatic movement is used with the mentally retarded children. Miss Iva Wonn, Director of the Christian Education Department of the Denver Area Council of Churches, writes:

One area in which this type of expression is particularly and uniquely helpful is with the mentally retarded who find it difficult to understand and use words. We are making more and more use of it in our church school classes for these children. While they cannot understand the words of the Lord's Prayer *in toto,* or of many of the hymns, we have been able to help them get the feeling of each phrase through the use of interpretive movement.

•   •   •

Joyce Peel, a leader in the Christian Drama Program in the Diocese of Madras in South India, tells of using Indian gestures in interpreting the Lord's Prayer:

We did it all kneeling. "Give us this day our daily bread" was shown by the cupping of hands as to receive the sacrament. "As we forgive others" was shown by the "Peace" gesture —the folding of the neighbor's hand in our own—which we use in the communion service of the Church of South India to represent our fellowship; taken originally from the Syrian Church. . . .

So with some variations I have taught the Lord's Prayer to children in the villages and to Hindus and to illiterates. They learn the prayer with the gestures.

This is only one of many references to the use of creative movement in the world ministry of the church. The ideas are interpreted by the symbolic gestures that have meaning to a particular people, but the language of movement would be understood even by a stranger. It is an ecumenical language of symbolic movement that children around the world may use as they express their discoveries of their relation to God and to others.

PART THREE

Creative Dramatic Movement
with Five-Seven year olds

Just Walking Is Meaningful

All around us worlds are dying and new worlds are being born;
All around us life is dying and life is being born.
The fruit ripens on the tree;
The roots are silently at work in the darkness of the earth
Against the time when there shall be new leaves, fresh blossoms,
green fruit.
Such is the growing edge!
It is the extra breath from the exhausted lung,
The one more thing to try when all else has failed,
The upward reach of life when weariness closes in upon
all endeavor.
This is the basis of hope in moments of despair,
The incentive to carry on when times are out of joint
And men have lost their reason, the source of confidence
When worlds crash and dreams whiten into ash.
The birth of a child—life's most dramatic answer to death—
This is the Growing Edge incarnate.
Look well to the growing edge!

—HOWARD THURMAN

10

CHILDREN WHO WALK IN JESUS' WAY

LEARNING A SONG THROUGH RHYTHMIC MOVEMENT

It is important for a child to learn to walk with assurance and joy (Figure 29). To walk with head high and a song in the heart will have as much value in mature years as in the first years of school.

Children enjoy walking as they sing "Children Who Walk in Jesus' Way."*

> Children who walk in Jesus' way
> Light shall go with them day by day.
> They shall be free, they shall be gay
> Children who walk in Jesus' way.

These words are set to a joyous folk tune, and the children will enjoy clapping the steady 4/4 beat while they are learning the song. The words can be printed or written in big letters on a large piece of paper or on a chalkboard.

Here are the suggested steps for using rhythmic movement in teaching a song:

Learn the Words and Music

Before the children walk to this song, they should be so familiar with the words that they will not need to read them. In fact, younger children will learn quickly from repetition without ever needing to see the words written out. Let them sing the words a few times until they know the song.

----

* Number 127 in *Hymns for Primary Worship*.

Clap the Rhythm

Suggest that the children clap the rhythm while they sing. As they sing and clap the third line, "They shall be free, they shall be gay," let them pause in their clapping and hold their hands open when they come to the words "free" and "gay," each of which is held for two beats.

Sense the Mood

Help the children to discover that this is a joyous song. Here you could show them the picture "Follow Me" by Tom Curr and ask them to notice how the children in the picture are smiling and how Jesus is smiling too.

Move About (walking, skipping, turning, singly and in groups)

Now the children are ready to walk and sing. At first they may walk about singly, singing, clapping, and smiling as they go. Another time they might try walking hand in hand in groups of two or three (Figure 30).

Introduce Variations

During the third line of the song the children could break away from each other and turn freely in any direction with a skip (Figure 31), a clap, or a spin, joining hands again on the last line, either with their previous partner or the child who happens to be nearest. They

FIGURE 29

FIGURE 31

FIGURE 30

then continue singing and walking together while they repeat the song once more.

The children themselves will have other variations to suggest.

Use Additional Background Material
(Lines from Scripture, Pictures)

Another day you might show the picture "The Hilltop at Nazareth" by Elsie Anna Wood, suggesting that Jesus, when he was about seven or eight years old, liked to walk on the hillsides above Nazareth. Perhaps another day some friends came walking up the hill with Jesus. The children may want to walk and clap, and sing the song again with this idea in mind.

Radiate Enthusiasm in Your Own Walk

The way you yourself walk is important to the children you teach, for they will reflect you. You need to speak to the children with your whole being. They will absorb your attitudes more clearly than the words you speak. You will need to practice walking with faith and joy all through the week. You need not feel that you must join with the children as they walk their song, but you will need the religious discipline that comes from a fusion of body, mind, and soul° if you are to help the children in your group to become radiant, enthusiastic persons in their own right.

° You will find help on this point in the author's book *Look Up and Live*, which is written for adults.

73

11

STOP, LOOK, AND WONDER

LEADER: Let's do some walking today. You can go anywhere about the room with a good free walk. I will clap my hands *(percussion or piano may be used instead)* steadily, 1-2-3-4, while you walk.

Swing your arms and look about, but don't look down. Here we go: 1-2-3-4—swing-your-arms-look-around-and stop! That stop light came all of a sudden, didn't it?

This time, instead of saying "Stop," I will say, "Oh, look at that beautiful rainbow!" *(Or play a melody with ascending and descending notes on the piano, autoharp, or xylophone).*

Think of the wide arch of a rainbow. Then trace it. Start very low (Figure 32), then with both arms stretch far out to the side and up, up, until you must come down on the other side.

Let's pretend that we dip our fingertips in a bowl at one side. That bowl is filled with all the colors of the rainbow. Now as we finger paint our rainbow in space, let those colors drip off your fingertips; the arch goes up—high—and then down in a wide curve. . . .

Good! Let's do it again and start from the opposite side this time. We'll paint a beautiful rainbow from its beginning to its height (Figure 33), and down to where it meets the earth. . . .

Now let's combine our walking and our rainbow. Walk to the steady beat, but when you hear, "Oh, look at that beautiful rainbow"

(or when you hear music), stop walking and finger paint a rainbow right in front of you wherever you are. Then walk about again, swinging your arms and looking around as if you didn't expect to see anything surprising until suddenly you hear the words, "Oh! look at that beautiful rainbow!" Then stop, swing the big curve, look up at the top of that arch before starting the downward curve on the other side.

Here we go: 1-2-3-4-1-2-3-4— Oh, look at that beautiful rainbow!

1-2-3-4-1-2-3-4-1-2-3-4— Oh, look at this beautiful rainbow!

1-2-3-4-1-2-3-4— Now, look at that beautiful rainbow!

1-2-3-4— Another beautiful rainbow!

Good! You were stretching up very high each time to make that rainbow in the sky.*

Now we'll do something a little different. But let's sit down and rest for a minute. . . .

We often walk about and don't take time to notice wonderful and surprising things. This time when we start walking as usual, instead of telling you to stop to look at a rainbow, I'll say: "Now there's something really wonderful!"

Each time we'll see something that we haven't taken time to think about before.

---

* The record Part I in *Let's Play Series,* Set II, recordings by Kay Ortman's, Box 2005, Ben Lomond, California, has original music for this activity.

74

While you look at it, reach toward it and outline its shape with your hands, or move the
way it does. You will be like a mirror. You
won't say what you're seeing in words, but
you'll be reflecting what it is or does through
the language of your body. (See Figures 34 and
35.)

Now let's start. Shut your eyes, and when
I count to three, open them and tell me what
you see. 1-2-3! . . .

What do you see? . . .

A picture? . . .

A clock? . . .

A table? . . .

*(Give the children time to study how each
thing is made, and to note its beauty or some
unique quality about it.)*

There are some beautiful and useful things
right here that we don't take time to think
about and enjoy. Let's take time now to think
deeply about some of these things. As we do,
we may decide that the people who made
them were wonderful for doing something
special. People seem to be created to create.

FIGURE 33

FIGURE 32

FIGURE 34

FIGURE 35

75

I believe we'll make some new discoveries today, so let's get up now and see what we can find. . . .

Here we go, walking first of all, 1-2-3-4-1-2-3-4. . . .

Now here's something beautiful, something really wonderful! . . . 1-2-3-4. . . . And here's something really wonderful!

(This is better when music or percussion is used to mark the contrasts, but it can be equally effective with clapping, counting, and exclamations on the part of the leader, as indicated.)

I wonder what you noticed. . . .

The record player? . . .

The big clear window? . . .

The tree outside the window? . . .

Scissors? . . .

Books? . . .

Those really are wonderful things.

You can play "Stop, Look, and Wonder" wherever you are—outdoors, in bed, on a porch, in church. You'll discover things you never even noticed before!

Time for Wonder

LEADER: Let's sit down now and get comfortable. . . .

We've been so busy seeing things, let's close our eyes and think deep inside ourselves. . . .

Let's think of rainbows that can come only when there is sunshine after a rain. Sometimes beautiful things happen when there have been stormy times. We can learn to "trace the rainbow through the rain" and look for the beautiful and wonderful. A rainbow has always been considered a promise of clear times ahead.

Now let's open our eyes as we think of all the beautiful and wonderful things that we have been noticing.

We can say a "thank-you" prayer to God, using our hands as well as our voices. Let's start with our hands together, . . . lift them in

wonder, . . . spread them apart and down, . . . and close them on the word "Amen." (See the illustrations for "A Thank-you Prayer," p. 27.)

I will say the words and you can repeat them after me and use your arms and hands to express the ideas:

Thank you God—*thank you God*—
For wonderful things—*for wonderful things*
Everywhere—*everywhere.*
Amen, *Amen.*

Notes for Leaders

Children enjoy walking and stopping to look at whatever catches their attention; this is a way to cultivate in children that sensitive awareness that is the beginning of joyous religious living. For accompaniment, you can clap the rhythm, use a drum, or play a march on the piano. If the children are imagining that they are looking at a rainbow, you may choose to speak the words, "Oh, look at that beautiful rainbow!" or to play a melody with ascending and descending notes on the piano, autoharp, or xylophone.

Before they actually walk about, the children may enjoy "walking" while sitting by striking the palms of their hands against their thighs in a walking rhythm, and then reaching up with their arms in a wide, high swinging arc. This will also involve a lifting of the head and diaphragm.

There are many songs that children will sing with greater understanding following an activity such as this that helps to increase awareness. "In Our Church We Like to Sing," Number 209 in *Sing to the Lord*, is especially good. Here are the words:

In our church we like to sing,
And sometimes we softly pray,
Thanking God for everything,
God who loves us every day.

12

CHANGE CHANTS

CHANGE OF MOODS
Act One: *No, I Won't*

LEADER: Do you ever say, "No, I won't!"? You do! Well, we all do. And sometimes we want to say it but don't.

Just for fun, let's say a chant together. Listen to the words first, and then repeat them after me.

> No, I won't!
> No, I won't!
> No—No—
> No, I won't!

(The children repeat the words with the leader.)

Say it again. This time, say it as if you really mean it.

(The children and the leader repeat the chant together. This time they give it more emphasis.)

Move about a bit, this time, while you say this chant. Say it with your whole self. Don't just say the words. . . .

Are you stamping for emphasis? . . .

Are your fists clenched? (Figure 36) . . .

Are you leaning forward with your chin sticking out? . . .

What are your elbows doing? . . .

Now say your chant wherever you turn. . . . Say it to the first person you see, . . . or to whatever you see. . . . Say it loudly and strongly, with every bit of yourself.

Here we go again:

> No, I won't!
> No, I won't!
> No—No—
> No, I won't!

What happens? . . .

Can you keep a grin from showing on your face? . . . I can't!

We all look silly and absurd. We are saying "No" in many different ways, and it is fun

FIGURE 36

because we don't exactly know what we are saying "No" about! It feels good to shout it out, though, and say it with carefree rudeness, because nobody here really minds!

Act Two: *Well, I Might!*

LEADER: Now let's see if we can make a bridge to take us away from our "no" feeling into a "yes" feeling. First, we can learn a new chant:

> Well, I might—
> Well, I might—
> I might not—
> And then I might!

(The children repeat the words with the leader, as in Act One.)

While we say this, let's stand in one place but look far away.

Over to the walls of the room. . . .

Out of the window. . . .

As far off as we can see. . . .

Even though our feet are in one place, our body can turn far around to one side and then far around to the other. . . . Each of us is like a tree that the wind blows one way and another, but the roots hold steady. . . .

(The children turn like trees blowing in the wind, while saying the chant.)

When you say, "I might not," you make it clear that *you* are the one who decides.

You can stand straight and tall. . . .

Or pull your chin in. . . .

Or turn your head to one side in a cocky way. . . .

Try out different ways (Figure 37). . . .

It's good to say, "I might not—" because then you feel freer to say, "And then—I might—" It is your choice.

Now let's repeat our chant:

> Well, I might—
> Well, I might—
> I might not—
> And then I might!

Act Three: *Yes, I Will!*

LEADER: Now we're ready to learn a different chant:

> Yes, I will!
> Yes, I will!
> Yes, I will!
> I certainly will!

(The children repeat the words with the leader as before.)

We can clap as we say this. One way to clap to show joy is to let your hands spring apart as soon as they have made a clap. Let's try it. . . . Let your hands feel that the clapping makes them fly apart! . . . When you say, "I certainly will!" the claps can go higher, so that at the end your hands fly apart above your head (Figure 38). Let's clap as we say our chant.

(The children repeat the chant while clapping.)

FIGURE 37

FIGURE 38

78

NO, I WON'T

WELL, I MIGHT

YES, I WILL

The music of this song is by Nina Cole.

79

Now let's skip, leap, or jump to show that we are happy. You can clap every once in a while, or just at the end when you give a high clap. . . . Or, you can make a high leap at the end. . . . Do what the chant makes you feel like doing. . . .

Here we go:

> Yes, I will!
> Yes, I will!
> Yes, I will!
> I certainly will!

LEADER: Now we are ready to do our three acts of "Change Chants," one right after the other.

First we'll do "No, I won't!" If you feel cross today, try to pour out that feeling in your "No" shouts.

Next we'll do "Well, I might." Here we make a bridge from "No, I won't!" to "Yes, I will!" So, we'll say, "Well, I might," rather softly.

Third, we'll do the "Yes, I will" act. Why, whatever was bothering us can be met with joy!

Here we go, now, with all three acts.

TIME FOR WONDER

LEADER: Every play has a beginning, a middle, and an end. How silly it would be if we did Act One over and over and never took time for Act Two. Next time you are feeling grouchy don't blame someone else. At first admit that you *are* grouchy.

Then something inside you says, "Let's see what we can do to get over this black mood." It may be that you will have to be very quiet and try to understand your trouble by looking far off or looking around.

And then comes Act Three when you decide to meet what you must. To say "Yes" is like stepping onto the first step of an escalator; then we go right up with very little effort. Say "Yes" to whatever is good and right and you will find that you are happier than before!

NOTES FOR LEADERS

In most homes today where young children are growing up, the adults of the family are apt to be rushed and tense, and impatient in correcting the child. Parents, grandparents, uncles, aunts, and even the older children pose a threat to the five-, six-, or seven-year-old, because they are all taller and stronger than he is.

The television, with its emotional dramas and news reports of world crises day after day, is another factor contributing to the tensions of the modern home.

Small wonder, then, if a child tends to drain off some of his own reflection of these tensions by irritating behavior only to succeed in bringing down upon himself more intense discipline. Obviously the young child needs some avenue of release for these tensions of his, some constructive outlet for his frustrations.

When a child needs a "drain-off" of pent-up, angry feelings, opportunity to exercise his natural drives to run or to gallop, or to skip to a drumbeat or other strongly rhythmic music will afford this needed avenue of release from bad feelings.

See Matthew 21:28-31a. In this Jesus knew how people may "say" "I will not" ("No, I won't") in one moment, yet change later.

Thanksgiving and Christmas

Children are capable of experiencing the
vibrant meaning of the symbolic movement of stretching
forth loving hands. When Isadora Duncan was asked how
she hoped to be able to teach any ordinary child to move
freely, she said she had "no systematic physical training, no
program of laborious technique." This she felt would develop
of itself by the constant exercise of the body in pursuit of
and in response to its motivating idea. . . . She then ex-
plained that there were children all over the world who,
though they spoke different languages and lived materially
separated lives, nevertheless . . . were all brothers and sisters. And the first gesture she asked them to make was to
reach forth their arms to these brothers and sisters with
only one idea in their minds, that this stretching forth of
arms was a greeting, a silent, far-reaching message of love.
Animated by this thought, and this thought alone, the gesture was always a beautiful one. It is amazing to see with
what grace the most untutored person will perform such a
gesture when actuated by this impelling mood, automati-
cally released from the awkward restraints of self-consciousness and the other impediments of habitual egoism. Whereas
if one were to set about making the same gracious movement by skill alone, uninspired by the urgency of the communication, the result might be what we call pretty but it
would not be beautiful.

—RICHARD GUGGENHEIMER

13

FOR THE BEAUTY OF THE EARTH

LEADER: Would you like to sing this hymn of praise with me? Perhaps you know it.

> For the beauty of the earth,
> For the glory of the skies,
> For the love which from our birth
> Over and around us lies.
> Lord of all, to thee we raise
> This our hymn of grateful praise.

This hymn gives us a group of pictures. We could draw them with our crayons, but right now, let's "finger paint" these pictures in space.

We'll say the first line softly, as we make our picture in space: "For the beauty of the earth"—we'll finger paint that first. Are you thinking of something especially beautiful? . . .

ALICE: I'm thinking of the flowers along the the edge of our garden. (*Kneels down, and reaches her hands forward and down.*)

KEVIN: I'm thinking of the grass just before it is cut—cool and green. (*Kneels also and holds his hands flat, moving them from side to side.*)

KAREN: I can see more of the earth if I am higher and turn around. (*Remains standing and turns to one side and then to the other, holding her arms out with the palms of her hands turned out; then also kneels.*) (See Figure 39.)

LEADER: There are so many ways to show that picture idea! Let's try the next one.

"For the glory of the skies." How would you express this in movement? Let's sing it softly as we experiment. . . .

(*This time the children move with greater ease and more variety.*)

Now you have some real ideas!

KEVIN: I'm a big telescope looking at the millions of stars. (*Holds his arms high and looks up as he turns around.*)

ALICE: It's a windy day and I'm watching the clouds float by. (*Holds her arms high, swaying them back and forth.*) (See Figure 40.)

KAREN: I'm thinking about a very clear, blue sky. I can't stretch far enough. (*Lifts her arms high and wide, but holds them very still.*)

LEADER: None of us can reach far enough, but you have all found wonderful ways of telling this idea. Let's sing that line again and try out a new way of showing it to see how it feels. There are so many ways to show the glory of sky, clouds, stars, space. . . .

Of course, each day is different, so each time we sing this line we can move in a different way if we want to. Let's sing it again as we try it out: "For the glory of the skies."

Now let's sing the next lines:

> For the love which from our birth
> Over and around us lies.

These lines describe an idea instead of a picture, so it is hard to show in movement. See what you can do. . . .

FIGURE 39

FIGURE 40

FIGURE 41

FIGURE 42

ALICE: (*Brings her arms down into a cradle position and looks down* [Figure 41]. *She rocks her arms gently back and forth.*)

KAREN: (*Folds her arms into a cradle position, but soon she pushes them up and lifts her head as she sings the word "over"* [Figure 42]. *She then lowers her arms sideward and down.*)

KEVIN: (*From turning to view the stars swings his arms out in a wide arc parallel to each other. Now, arms still parallel, he swoops them out to one side and down. Then he raises them high on the other side, over his head and down again. He has made more than a full circle with his arms.*)

LEADER: Good. You were all showing how love is all about us from the very start. Let's sing this line again and see what new ideas come to us, or else repeat what we just did, to see if it feels good to us.

 For the love which from our birth
 Over and around us lies.

83

Those were splendid wide and circling movements.

Come, let's sit down and look at this drawing of a Celtic cross.* The cross stands for Christ. This Celtic cross has a circle in the center. Do you know what the circle represents? It is a symbol for eternity. It means "now and forever." When we think of love in an endless circle, part of that love is in our parents, our friends, and ourselves, but a much larger part of it is the never-ending love that God has for each of us.

KAREN: What if we do wrong? Does the circle get broken?

LEADER: Jesus tells us that God loves us even when we do wrong—but Jesus also tells us that to be really happy we should admit our mistakes and start afresh to do right. God's love is forever and for each of us. So you see, the circle does not really get broken.

KAREN: Let's do the rest of our song, but let's start from the beginning.

LEADER: A good idea!

(They sing the stanza and interpret it.)

Now we've come to our last lines. Let's sing them:

> Lord of all, to thee we raise
> This our hymn of grateful praise.

What do you suppose "Lord of all" means?

KEVIN: It means that God is the creator of everything about us.

KAREN: It might mean that God is the Lord of all people and that he wants everyone to enjoy flowers, stars, mothers, and good things like that.

LEADER: It could mean either one or both of those ideas. Do you think "all" could mean

people in faraway countries as well as people we know? Let's try showing what "Lord of all" means.

KEVIN: I'm stretching my arms out wide as they'll go—for everyone (Figure 43).

KAREN: I'm turning around, thinking of people all around the world.

ALICE: God does so many things that we can't do, so I feel like bowing very low.

LEADER: Let's go right on to the next part, "to thee we raise." That means we should reach up, doesn't it?

ALICE: Or look up.

LEADER: Yes, and it links right into the next line:

> This our hymn of grateful praise.

How shall we express our thankful praise? It is not easy. Let's take some time to try it. . . . What did you figure out?

KEVIN: I decided to spread my arms out wide and high and be like a loud-speaker sending out a song of thanks (Figures 43 and 44).

ALICE: Well, since I have been down low on "Lord of all," I'll just keep going higher and higher, very slowly, all the way to the end.

KAREN: I'm pretending that I've gathered all my thanks as a gift—right here in my hands—to give to God because of all the gifts God has given me. That's why I'm lifting my hands this way.

LEADER: Those are all good ways of saying our thanks. Let's all sit down here for a minute. . . . When you receive a wonderful gift on your birthday, can you keep from smiling as you say, "Oh, thank you!"? Hardly! If you are really thankful it shows on your face! Smiling is as important as lifting your arms in this song of praise. Sitting right here, let's sing those lines smiling:

---

* The Celtic cross is illustrated and interpreted in *Our Christian Symbols* by Friedrich Rest, published by the Christian Education Press.

Lord of all, to thee we raise
This our hymn of grateful praise.

Now let's show the whole hymn in any way we want to, as we use our body, mind, and soul—every bit of ourselves—in praise to God.

If you follow the sequence of movements that each child evolves individually, you will see that Alice has a sequence that flows in a related manner; and that Karen and Kevin each has his own sequence of movements.

FIGURE 43

FIGURE 44

14

PSALM 100

Psalm 100 is a psalm of thanksgiving that is well adapted for use with younger children. It lends itself to a harvest home or Thanksgiving festival, but is also appropriate for any worship service as an expression of the moods of thanksgiving and humble waiting before the Lord. Thanksgiving is any time and all the time, and children enjoy expressing their thankfulness through dramatic movement.

Make a joyful noise unto the Lord, unto the Lord,
All ye lands, all ye lands,
Serve the Lord with gladness, serve the Lord with gladness.
Come before his presence with singing.

Know ye that the Lord, he is God;
It is he that hath made us, and not we ourselves.

Make a joyful noise unto the Lord, unto the Lord,
All ye lands, all ye lands,
Serve the Lord with gladness, serve the Lord with gladness,
Come before his presence with singing.

This arrangement of Psalm 100:1-3, prepared and set to music by Carl Mueller,* may be in-

* Mueller, Carl: *The 100th Psalm*. (No. 86032). Published by Harold Flammer, New York. The portion of this anthem suggested for use here includes all of pages 2 and 3 and the first three bars on page 4, sung in unison instead of two parts.

terpreted with very simple movements as follows:

The children may speak the words of this psalm in unison, as they move in response to the ideas it presents. Several children may provide a background of "joyful noise" with percussion instruments (Figure 45), or the group may learn to sing the psalm in this musical arrangement, and move to the ideas it presents as they sing.

During the first four lines the children may choose to walk forward in ones and twos in joyous processional. Some may play percussion instruments. Some may carry gifts of fruits and vegetables in wooden bowls and baskets, and gifts of fall flowers and bright leaves, and place these as harvest home gifts on a central table.

During the lines:

Know ye that the Lord, he is God;
It is he that hath made us, and not we ourselves.

the children sing or speak softly and reverently as they kneel to express feelings of humility and reverence (Figures 46 and 47). Percussion instruments would be still during these lines. With the last four lines the children may return to their mood of joyful noise in a recessional.

The children will be quick to grasp the contrast of joyous movement and quiet humility as they interpret this psalm.

FIGURE 45

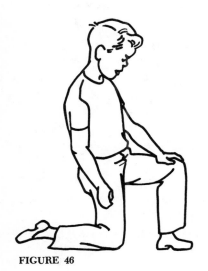

FIGURE 46

FIGURE 47

15

STARS AT CHRISTMAS TIME

LEADER: How we all love to sing Christmas carols. In one of the carols that Martin Luther wrote for children to sing around a Christmas crèche there is this stanza:

> I can play the whole day long,
> I'll dance and sing for you a song,
> A soft and soothing lullaby
> So sweet that you will never cry.*

We might "dance and sing" a carol to show our joy at Christmas time. We've been making stars for Christmas decorations (Figure 48). Let's be Christmas stars ourselves. Let's be like the stars that shone on that first Christmas when Jesus was born. We all know the carol "O Little Town of Bethlehem." Let's sing it and think of stars as we sing. Whenever we sing "stars," let's raise our hands for a moment, but keep right on singing. . . .

(If the children do not know the first two stanzas of "O Little Town of Bethlehem" you could have the words printed clearly on the blackboard or on a large sheet of paper propped up on an easel, where the children can read them easily.)

GROUP *(sings in unison):*

> O little town of Bethlehem,
> How still we see thee lie;

---

* From "From Heaven High," translated by Roland Bainton, p. 90 in *The Whole World Singing*.

> Above thy deep and dreamless sleep
> The silent *stars* go by.
> Yet in thy dark streets shineth
> The everlasting Light;
> The hopes and fears of all the years
> Are met in thee tonight.

> For Christ is born of Mary,
> And gathered all above,
> While mortals sleep,
> The angels keep
> Their watch of wondering love.
> O morning stars, together
> Proclaim the holy birth!
> And praises sing to God the King,
> And peace to men on earth!

LEADER: Good! You noticed each time you sang about the stars. Now what shall we do if we are to be like the stars in this carol? We need a lot of ideas. . . .

KAREN: I can wrap my baby doll in a blanket and lay it on this low table.

KEVIN: What does that have to do with stars?

KAREN: That's the baby Jesus for the stars to shine on.

JOHN: Let's use the stars we have been making. We can take the stars far off first, and then start moving very slowly and quietly toward Bethlehem.

JANET: I think we could kneel down and hold

FIGURE 48—To Make Sparkling Stars

These stars should be about six inches in diameter.

Trace star on page 71 and copy on cardboard. You may cover the cardboard with gilt paper or use gold paint. When the stars are cut out sprinkle them with bits of gold sparkle.

To allow the star to hang from your finger, thread a wire hook, such as those used for Christmas tree ornaments, or pull a loop of thread, through a small hole pierced in one of the points of the star.

our stars up for the baby to look at when we get close. Then we can move away and let someone else have a turn.

JOHN: When we sing "and gathered all above," we should all be together then.

KEVIN: I don't think we need to be together until we sing,

> O morning stars, together
> Proclaim the holy birth.

Then we can all be together and hold our stars up high.

LEADER: Why don't we try out some of these ideas? Then we can see just when we feel we should gather together.

KAREN: I'll put my sweater here, to make a bed for the baby Jesus.

JOHN: Come on over to this corner so we'll have a long way to come.

KEVIN: Why don't we use two corners?

JOHN: That's O.K. It's just as far from that corner.

FIGURE 49

(*The children all sing, moving forward slowly and holding their stars out before them* [Figure 49]. *They agree that the time to be together is when they sing the line "O morning stars together."*)

89

FIGURE 50

KAREN: Does "proclaim" mean *announce?*

JANET: Yes, it means something like a news broadcast.

JOHN: We can hold our stars up high to broadcast the news that Jesus is born (Figure 50).

KAREN: And we can lower them when we sing, "And peace to men on earth!"

KEVIN: Let's hum instead of singing while we go back to our corners.

LEADER: These are all splendid ideas! Let's put them all together now. First we find our star-homes and start out. . . .

We'll come in slowly, perhaps kneel by the baby, and move on until we come together and lift our stars high as we sing:

> O morning stars, together
> Proclaim the holy birth.

We lower them as we sing, "And peace to men on earth." Then we hum softly as we return to our star-homes.

(The children sing the carol and interpret it with reverence and absorbed attention. Everyone is free from self-consciousness, concentrating on the role of Christmas star.)

LEADER: That is beautiful! Let's sit down together for a few minutes and tell what we liked the best. . . .

JANET: I liked coming in—I felt as if something surprising was happening. I liked kneeling for a minute too.

KEVIN: I liked turning like a planet when we were going back to our star-homes. I don't like to think of words, so I liked the humming part.

JOHN: I liked lifting my star up high, and I had mine higher than any of the others!

KAREN: I think we should have Mary taking care of the baby. May I be Mary if we do it again?

LEADER: We will do this again; if not right now, when we meet next week. Perhaps then you'll have even more ideas for "dancing and singing" this carol.

NOTES FOR LEADERS

The purpose of the stars is twofold. They serve as a springboard for this interpretation of "O Little Town of Bethlehem," but more important is the fact that to hold a star helps a child to be less self-conscious. He becomes absorbed in what he holds and what he does with it, and is thus able to forget himself.

Resources

and Acknowledgements

RESOURCES

BOOKS

A Time To Dance by Margaret Taylor. Sharing Company, 1976.
Children Discover Music and Dance by Emma D. Sheehy. Henry Holt, 1959.
Creative Dance for Children by Marcia Eastman. Mettler Studios, 1954. Available from Barbara Mettler, Box 4456, Tucson, Ariz.
Creative Rhythmic Movement for Children by Gladys Andrews. Prentice-Hall, 1954.
Creative Teaching in the Church by Eleanor Shelton Morrison and Virgil E. Foster. Prentice-Hall, 1963.
Dance in Elementary Education by Ruth Lovell Murray. Harper and Brothers, 1953.
The Educational Mission of Our Church by Roger Lincoln Shinn. United Church Press, 1962.
Leap to Life by John Wiles and Alan Garrard. London: Chatto and Windus, 1957.
Let's Play by LaDonna Bogardus. National Council of the Churches of Christ, 1958.
Look Up and Live by Margaret Palmer Fisk. *The Sharing Company, 1977*
Materials of Dance as a Creative Art Activity by Barbara Mettler. Mettler Studios, 1960. Available from Barbara Mettler, Box 4456, Tucson, Ariz.
The Power of Dance by Madeleine Dixon. John Day, 1939.
Psychology of Religion by Laurence W. Grenstead. Oxford University Press, 1952.
Religious Dances in the Christain Church and in Popular Medicine by E. Louis Backman. London: Allen and Unwin, 1952.
Time for Wonder by Margaret Fisk Taylor. United Church Press (The Christian Education Press), 1961.

Using Movement Creatively in Religious Education by Pat Sonen. Unitarian Universalist Association, 1963.

ARTICLES

"The Bible into Life Through Symbolic Movement" by Margaret Palmer Fisk in *International Journal of Religious Education* (November 1955).
"Boys at Work" by Betty Smith in *Dance Magazine* (March 1962).
"Boys Will *Still* Be Boys" by Marva Spelman in *Dance Magazine* (August 1957).
"Creative Dance and the Child" by Bonnie Bird in *Dance Magazine* (October 1958).
"Creative Dance for Children" by Lucile Brahms Nathanson in *Dance Magazine* (August, October, December 1955).
"Creative Movement in the Christian Education of Children" by Margaret Fisk Taylor in *International Journal of Religious Education* (April 1961).
"Creative Rhythmic Movement as a Religious Education Art" by Margaret Fisk Taylor in *Religious Education* (January–February 1958).
"Dance Is Discovery" by Bernice Rosen in *Dance Magazine* (June 1961).
"A Feeling of Reality" by Carol M. Warner in *Children's Religion* (June 1958).
"Music for Juniors" by Norma Lowder in *Music Ministry* (April 1963).
"Rhythmic Movement in Christian Education" by Martha Cornick in *International Journal of Religious Education* (April 1957).
"Roots and Wings" by Virginia Tanner in *Dance Magazine* (November 1963).
"Symbiosis: Pasadena Art Museum and Dance

Class" by Hilda Mullin and Vilma Potter in *Dance Magazine* (February 1963).

"The Use of Creative Drama with Children" by Eleanor Shelton Morrison and Virgil E. Foster in *International Journal of Religious Education* (September 1963).

"Virginia Tanner Teaches" by Robert Bruce Bennett in *Dance Magazine* (June 1955).

"Who Is a Creative Teacher?" by Grace Stanistreet in *Dance Magazine* (February 1962).

FILMSTRIPS

The following filmstrips on the use of Creative Dramatic Movement with children directed by Margaret Fisk Taylor have scripts for children's viewing and instructional scripts for leaders, written by Mrs. Taylor. The filmstrips were produced by Ruth Lister and are available from :
The Sharing Company.

Number 4—The story of the good Samaritan and "Joshua Fought the Battle of Jericho."

Number 5—Psalm 100, planets, "This Is My Father's World," and "Deck the Halls."

Number 6—Relatedness to another, a lonely one and a group, and "The Holly and the Ivy."

Number 7—"Jesus Walked This Lonesome Valley," and "In Christ There Is No East or West."

Number 8—"Praise and Thanksgiving" and "All Creatures of Our God and King."

SONG BOOKS

Handy Play Party Book; Little Book of Carols; Look Away: 50 Negro Folk Songs; Sing a Tune; Cooperative Recreation Service, Delaware, Ohio.

The Oxford Book of Carols by Percy Dearmer, R. Vaughn Williams, and Martin Shaw. Oxford University Press, 1928.

Sing for Joy, compiled and edited by Norman and Margaret Mealy. Seabury Press, 1961.

The Whole World Singing, compiled by Edith Lovell Thomas. Friendship Press, 1950.

ACKNOWLEDGMENTS

Page 7: "Christian learning involves participation"

From *The Educational Mission of Our Church* by Roger Lincoln Shinn, p. 54. United Church Press, 1962.

Page 9: "The key to guiding [the] child"

From "Roots and Wings" by Virginia Tanner in *Dance Magazine* (November 1963), p. 16.

Page 11: "When you utter a word"

From *Martin Buber: Jewish Existentialist* by Malcolm Diamond, p. 95. Oxford University Press, 1960.

Page 11: "There is measure in everything"

From *Much Ado About Nothing* by William Shakespeare.

Page 12: "All children will experience"

From "Music for Juniors" by Norma Lowder in *Music Ministry* (April 1963), p. 39. Graded Press.

Page 13: "Be adventurous"

From *Using Movement Creatively in Religious Education* by Pat Sonen, p. 37. Unitarian Universalist Association, 1963.

Page 13: "The boys and girls thought"

From *Children Discover Music and Dance* by Emma D. Sheehy, p. 180. Copyright © 1959, Holt, Rinehart & Winston, Inc. By permission.

Page 14: "What the teacher is"

From "Who Is a Creative Teacher?" by Grace Stanistreet in *Dance Magazine* (February 1962), pp. 46-47.

Page 15: "Why use only your speaking voice"

From *Let's Play* by LaDonna Bogardus, pp. 24, 28, 21. Published by the National Council of Churches. Copyright 1958. Used with permission.

Page 20: "All nature sings, and round me rings"

From "This Is My Father's World" by Maltbie D. Babcock.

Page 20: "Many of the ancient peoples"

From "Old Beliefs Persist in Starry Music" by J. Hugh Pruett in *Post Intelligencer* (Seattle, Wash.), October 17, 1953.

Page 23: "This is my Father's world"

From "This Is My Father's World" by Maltbie D. Babcock.

Page 24: "Jane Crofut"

From *Our Town* by Thornton Wilder, p. 54. Coward McCann, Inc., 1938.

Page 24: "Some things there are which make me know"

"Some Things There Are" by William L. Stidger in *Choral Readings for Junior Worship and Inspiration*, edited by Helen A. Brown and Harry J. Heltman, pp. 42-43. Westminster Press, 1957. Used by permission of Elizabeth Stidger Hyland.

Page 37: "Joy to the world, the Lord is come"

From "Joy to the World" by Isaac Watts.

93

Page 40: "What more natural thing"
From *Ultimate Questions* by Nathaniel Micklem. Abingdon Press, 1955.

Page 41: "Religion has suffered"
From "Dancing Party" by Simeon Stylites in *The Christian Century* (April 27, 1960), p. 527. Copyright 1960, Christian Century Foundation. Reprinted by permission.

Page 42: "Christian learning involves participation" and "Persons face each other"
From *The Educational Mission of Our Church* by Roger Lincoln Shinn, pp. 54, 104. United Church Press, 1962.

Page 44: "Push the protoplasmic paw out into space"
From "Amoeba Proteus" by Winifred Duncan in *Main Currents* (Spring 1949).

Page 44: "I stand at the seashore"
From "The Value of Science" by Richard P. Feynman in *Engineering and Science* (December 1955).

Page 45: "If posture is a gesture toward life"
From "Posture: A Gesture Toward Life" by Douglas Gordon Campbell in *Physiotherapy Review* (Vol. 15, No. 2, 1935).

Page 47: "When the class was expressing grief"
From *Using Movement Creatively in Religious Education* by Pat Sonen, p. 18. Unitarian Universalist Association, 1963.

Page 50: "To provide for an opportunity"
From *Using Movement Creatively in Religious Education* by Pat Sonen, p. 12. Unitarian Universalist Association, 1963.

Page 53: "Sometimes it takes lots of talk"
From *Using Movement Creatively in Religious Education* by Pat Sonen, pp. 24-25. Unitarian Universalist Association, 1963.

Page 56: "For the beauty of the earth"
From "For the Beauty of the Earth" by Folliott S. Pierpoint. Copyright words reprinted by permission of the Executors of the Estate of the late F. S. Pierpoint and Oxford University Press, London.

Page 63: "Now the green blade riseth"
From *The Oxford Book of Carols* by Percy Dearmer, R. Vaughn Williams, and Martin Shaw, p. 301. London: Oxford University Press, 1928.

Page 64: "On Easter Day"
From *Religious Dances in the Christian Church and in Popular Medicine* by E. Louis Backman, p. 75. London: George Allen & Unwin, 1952.

Page 66: "Alleluia, Alleluia, shout the news to all the earth"
From "An Easter Carol" by Helen C. Rockfeller in *Church Music Review* (Number 1966). Copyright 1946 by The H. W. Gray Co., Inc. Used by permission.

Page 67: "Christ the Lord is risen today"
From "Christ the Lord Is Risen Today" by Charles Wesley.

Page 67: "Four girls were selected"
From "A Feeling of Reality" by Carol M. Warner in *Children's Religion* (June 1958) pp. 16-17.

Page 67: "Must not be considered solely"
From *Psychology of Religion* by Laurence W. Grenstead. Oxford University Press, 1952.

Page 71: "All around us worlds are dying"
   From *The Growing Edge* by Howard Thurman, frontispiece. Harper and Brothers, 1956.

Page 72: "Children who walk in Jesus' way"
   Adapted from "Children Who Walk in Jesus' Way" by Nancy Bryd Turner in *Song and Play for Children* by Danielson and Conant, Pilgrim Press, 1953. Also Number 127 in *Hymns for Primary Worship*. Westminster Press, 1946.

Page 76 "In our church we like to sing"
   "In Our Church We Like to Sing" in *When They Are Three* by Elizabeth Cringan Gardner. Copyright 1950, by W. L. Jenkins, Westminster Press. Also Number 209 in *Sing to the Lord*. Christian Education Press, 1959.

Page 81: "Children are capable of experiencing"
   From *Sight and Insight* by Richard Guggenheimer. Harper and Brothers, 1945.

Page 82 "For the beauty of the earth"
   Adapted from "For the Beauty of the Earth." Used by permission of the Estate of the late Folliott Sanford Pierpont and the Oxford University Press, London. Number 10 in *Sing to the Lord*. Christian Education Press, 1959.

Page 88 "I can play the whole day long"
   From *The Martin Luther Christmas Book*. Translated by Roland Bainton. Copyright 1948, by W. L. Jenkins, Westminster Press. Also in *The Whole World Singing*, compiled by Edith Lovell Thomas, p. 90. Friendship Press, 1950.

The following publications are available from The Sharing Co.,
P.O.Box 2224, Austin, Texas 78768-2224. Send checks for orders
plus $1 for postage and handling.

Adams, <u>CONGREGATIONAL DANCING IN CHRISTIAN WORSHIP</u>, 161pp.$4.95

Adams, <u>DANCING CHRISTMAS CAROLS</u>, 132pp.$6.95

Adams, <u>HUMOR IN THE AMERICAN PULPIT</u>, 245pp.$6.95

Adams, <u>MEETING HOUSE TO CAMP MEETING</u>, 160pp.$6.95

Adams, <u>INVOLVING PEOPLE IN DANCING WORSHIP</u>, 23pp.$1.75

Bellamak, <u>NON-JUDGMENTAL SACRED DANCE</u>, 23pp.$2.50

Fisher, <u>DANCING THE OLD TESTAMENT</u>, 128pp.$5.95

Fisher, <u>MUSIC & DANCE IN WORSHIP</u>, 20pp.$2.50

Irwin, <u>PRIMER OF PRAYER GESTURE</u>, 30pp.$3.00

Kirk, <u>MEXICAN & NATIVE AMERICAN DANCES IN WORSHIP</u>, 30pp.$3.00

Lyon, <u>DANCE TOWARD WHOLENESS: HEALING MOVEMENTS</u>, 108pp.$5.95

MacLeod, <u>DANCING THROUGH PENTECOST</u>, 35pp.$3.00

Reed, <u>AND WE HAVE DANCED: SACRED DANCE 1958-1978</u>, 210pp.$5.95

Rock, <u>THEOLOGY IN THE SHAPE OF DANCE: DANCE IN WORSHIP</u>,27pp.$2

Rock&Adams, <u>BIBLICAL CRITERIA IN MODERN DANCE</u>, 16pp.$2.50

Seaton, <u>SCRIPTURAL CHOREOGRAPHY:DANCE FORMS IN WORSHIP</u>, 21pp.$2.50

Sonen, <u>USING MOVEMENT CREATIVELY IN CHRISTIAN EDUCATION</u>,38pp.$3.00

Taussig, <u>THE LADY OF THE DANCE: DANCING BIBLICAL WISDOM</u>,24pp.$2.50

Taussig, <u>NEW CATEGORIES FOR DANCING THE OLD TESTAMENT</u>, 28pp.$2.50

Taussig, <u>DANCING THE NEW TESTAMENT</u>, 12pp.$2.00

Taylor, <u>CONSIDERATIONS FOR STARTING & STRETCHING DANCE CHOIR</u>, $2.75

Taylor, <u>CREATIVE MOVEMENT:STEPS TOWARD UNDERSTANDING</u>,12pp.$2.00

Taylor, <u>DRAMATIC DANCE WITH CHILDREN IN WORSHIP & ED.</u>, 96pp.$4.95

Taylor, <u>LOOK UP AND LIVE: DANCE AS PRAYER & MEDITATION</u>,96pp.$4.95

Taylor, <u>A TIME TO DANCE: SYMBOLIC MOVEMENT IN WORSHIP</u>, 192pp.$5.95

Trolin, <u>MOVEMENT IN PRAYER IN A HASIDIC MODE</u>, 14pp.$2.50

Verbel, <u>DANCE & PRAYER:METHODS WITH HIGH SCHOOL STUDENTS</u>, 9pp$2.50

Yates, <u>FINANCING A SACRED DANCE CHOIR</u>, 56pp.$3.00

Send check for total order plus $1 for postage & handling to
"The Sharing Company," P.O.Box 2224, Austin, Texas 78768-2224.